The World's Famous Orations

VOL. VIII

AMERICA—I

1761—1837

THE WORLD'S FAMOUS ORATIONS

WILLIAM JENNINGS BRYAN
EDITOR-IN-CHIEF

FRANCIS W. HALSEY
ASSOCIATE EDITOR

IN TEN VOLUMES

Vol. VIII
AMERICA—I

FUNK *and* **WAGNALLS COMPANY**
New York and London

CONTENTS

CONTENTS

VOL. VIII
AMERICA—I
1761—1837

NORTH AMERICAN INDIANS

I

LOGAN TO LORD DUNMORE[1]
(1774)

Born about 1725, died in 1780; his real name, Tahgahjute; by birth a Cayuga, but made a Chief of the Mingoes; lived for many years in western Pennsylvania; his family murdered by the whites in 1774; killed near Detroit in a skirmish with Indians.

I APPEAL to any white man to say if ever he entered Logan's cabin hungry, and he gave him not meat; if ever he came cold and naked, and he clothed him not. During the course of the last long and bloody war Logan remained idle in his cabin, an advocate for peace. Such was my love for the whites that my countrymen pointed at me as they passed, and said: "Logan is the friend of white men."

I had even thought to have lived with you, but

---

[1] Lord Dunmore at this time was governor of Virginia. Logan's speech was really a message sent to Dunmore by Logan through John Gibson, an Indian trader. There was war at that time between the Indians and whites on the western frontier of Virginia. Trouble had long existed in that region, but the killing of Logan's family had now become the immediate cause of a general outbreak. The war was brought to a close on October 10 by the Battle of Point Pleasant, in which Logan is said personally to have taken thirty scalps.

for the injuries of one man. Colonel Cresap,[1] the last spring, in cold blood and unprovoked, murdered all the relations of Logan, not sparing even my women and children. There runs not a drop of my blood in the veins of any living creature.

This called on me for revenge. I have sought it. I have killed many. I have glutted my vengeance. For my country, I rejoice at the beams of peace. But do not think that mine is the joy of fear. Logan never felt fear. Logan will not turn on his heel to save his life. Who is there to mourn for Logan? Not one!

[1] Colonel Michael Cresap, after whom this war has sometimes been named, tho it is more often called Lord Dunmore's War, was not responsible for the murder of Logan's family. Some white men, led by one Greathouse, a liquor dealer, murdered them.

II

BRANT TO LORD GEORGE GERMAINE[1]
(1776)

Born in 1742, died in 1807; educated at Lebanon, Connecticut; Interpreter and Secretary to Sir William Johnson; visited London in 1776 and 1784; commanded the Indians at the battles of Oriskany and Newtown; translated parts of the New Testament into the Mohawk tongue; his life has been written in a notable book by William L. Stone.

BROTHER GORAH:—We have crossed the great lake and come to this kingdom with our superintendent, Colonel Johnson,[2] from our Confederacy of the Six Nations and their allies, that we might see our father, the great king, and join in informing him, his counselors, and wise men, of the good intentions of the Indians, our brothers, and of their attachment to his majesty and his government.

[1] Delivered in London before Lord George Germaine, secretary of state, on March 14, 1776. The originals of this and another speech by Brant are now in London. They have been printed in the "Documents Relating to the Colonial History of New York." Brant had gone to London to secure for the Mohawk Indians redress for lands which they had lost on the Mohawk and Upper Susquehanna Rivers. Redress was promised, but it was understood that the Indians meanwhile, in the war already begun with the Colonies, would give their support to the king. Out of this understanding proceeded the activity of Brant on the New York frontier in aid of the royal cause.

[2] Colonel Guy Johnson, who two years before (in 1774) had succeeded Sir William Johnson as superintendent of Indian affairs. He was not Sir William's son, but his son-in-law.

5

Brother, the disturbances in America give great trouble to all our nations, and many strange stories have been told to us by the people of that country. The Six Nations, who always loved the king, sent a number of their chiefs and warriors with their superintendent to Canada last summer, where they engaged their allies to join with them in the defense of that country, and when it was invaded by the New England people they alone defeated them.[1]

Brother, in that engagement we had several of our best warriors killed and wounded, and the Indians think it very hard they should have been so deceived by the white people in that country; many returning in great numbers, and no white people supporting the Indians, they were obliged to return to their villages and sit still. We now, brother, hope to see these bad children chastised, and that we may be enabled to tell the Indians who have always been faithful and ready to assist the king what his majesty intends.

Brother, the Mohawks, our particular nation, have on all occasions shown their zeal and loyalty to the great king; yet they have been very badly treated by the people in that country, the city of Albany laying an unjust claim to the

---

[1] A reference to General Montgomery's expedition to Quebec in the summer of 1775, and particularly to the Battle of the Cedars, fought near Montreal on September 25, where Ethan Allen, with a small force, was defeated, taken prisoner, and sent to England in the same ship in which Brant sailed.

lands on which our lower castle [1] is built, as one Klock,[2] and others do to those of Canajoharie, our upper village. We have often been assured by our late great friend, Sir William Johnson, who never deceived us, and we know he was told so, that the king and wise men here would do us justice. But this, notwithstanding all our applications, has never been done, and it makes us very uneasy. We also feel for the distress in which our brothers on the Susquehanna are likely to be involved by a mistake made in the boundary we settled in 1768.[3] This also our superintendent has laid before the king. We have only, therefore, to request that his majesty will attend to this matter: it troubles our nation and they can not sleep easy in their beds. Indeed, it is very hard, when we have let the king's subjects have so much land for so little value, they should want to cheat us in this manner of the small spots we have left for our women and children to live on. We are tired out in making complaints and getting no redress. We therefore hope that the assurances now given us by the superintendent may take place and that he may have it in his power to procure us justice.

[1] The lower castle of the Mohawks was at Fort Hunter.

[2] George Klock, of Canajoharie, was the father-in-law of Colonel Cox, who was killed at Oriskany. Cox was largely responsible at Oriskany for the injudicious forward movement of the American troops, which led them into an ambush laid by the Indians under Brant.

[3] At the Treaty of Fort Stanwix.

We shall truly report all that we hear from you to the Six Nations on our return. We are well informed there have been many Indians in this country who came without any authority from their own and gave us much trouble. We desire to tell you, brother, that this is not our case. We are warriors known to all the Nations, and are now here by approbation of many of them, whose sentiments we speak.

Brother, we hope that these things will be considered and that the king or his great men will give us such answer as will make our hearts light and glad before we go, and strengthen our hands, so that we may join our superintendent, Colonel Johnson, in giving satisfaction to all our Nations when we report to them on our return; for which purpose we hope soon to be accommodated with the passage.

III

RED JACKET ON THE RELIGION OF THE WHITE MAN AND THE RED [1]

(1805)

Born about 1752, died in 1830; his Nation, the Senecas, his home, near Geneva; his real name, Sogoyewapha, the name "Red Jacket" coming from an embroidered scarlet jacket presented to him by a British officer during the Revolution; saw service on the American side in the War of 1812.

FRIEND AND BROTHER:—It was the will of the Great Spirit that we should meet together this day. He orders all things and has given us a fine day for our council. He has taken His garment from before the sun and caused it to shine with brightness upon us. Our eyes are opened that we see clearly; our ears are unstopped that we have been able to hear distinctly the words you have spoken. For all these favors we thank the Great Spirit, and Him only.

Brother, this council fire was kindled by you. It was at your request that we came together at this time. We have listened with attention to what you have said. You requested us to speak our minds freely. This gives us great joy; for we now consider that we stand upright before you and can speak what we think. All have

[1] Delivered at a council of chiefs of the Six Nations in the summer of 1805 after Mr. Cram, a missionary, had spoken of the work he proposed to do among them.

heard your voice and all speak to you now as one man. Our minds are agreed.

Brother, you say you want an answer to your talk before you leave this place. It is right you should have one, as you are a great distance from home and we do not wish to detain you. But first we will look back a little and tell you what our fathers have told us and what we have heard from the white people.

Brother, listen to what we say. There was a time when our forefathers owned this great island. Their seats extended from the rising to the setting sun. The Great Spirit had made it for the use of Indians. He had created the buffalo, the deer, and other animals for food. He had made the bear and the beaver. Their skins served us for clothing. He had scattered them over the country and taught us how to take them. He had caused the earth to produce corn for bread. All this He had done for His red children because He loved them. If we had some disputes about our hunting-ground they were generally settled without the shedding of much blood.

But an evil day came upon us. Your forefathers crossed the great water and landed on this island. Their numbers were small. They found friends and not enemies. They told us they had fled from their own country for fear of wicked men and had come here to enjoy their religion. They asked for a small seat. We took pity on them, granted their request, and they sat down among us. We gave them corn and meat; they gave us poison in return.

The white people, brother, had now found our country. Tidings were carried back and more came among us. Yet we did not fear them. We took them to be friends. They called us brothers. We believed them and gave them a larger seat. At length their numbers had greatly increased. They wanted more land; they wanted our country. Our eyes were opened and our minds became uneasy. Wars took place. Indians were hired to fight against Indians, and many of our people were destroyed. They also brought strong liquor among us. It was strong and powerful, and has slain thousands.

Brother, our seats were once large and yours were small. You have now become a great people, and we have scarcely a place left to spread our blankets. You have got our country, but are not satisfied; you want to force your religion upon us.

Brother, continue to listen. You say that you are sent to instruct us how to worship the Great Spirit agreeably to His mind; and, if we do not take hold of the religion which you white people teach we shall be unhappy hereafter. You say that you are right and we are lost. How do we know this to be true? We understand that your religion is written in a Book. If it was intended for us, as well as you, why has not the Great Spirit given to us, and not only to us, but why did He not give to our forefathers the knowledge of that Book, with the means of understanding it rightly. We only know what you tell us about it. How shall we know when to believe, being so often deceived by the white people?

Brother, you say there is but one way to worship and serve the Great Spirit. If there is but one religion, why do you white people differ so much about it? Why not all agreed, as you can all read the Book?

Brother, we do not understand these things. We are told that your religion was given to your forefathers and has been handed down from father to son. We also have a religion which was given to our forefathers and has been handed down to us, their children. We worship in that way. It teaches us to be thankful for all the favors we receive, to love each other, and to be united. We never quarrel about religion.

Brother, the Great Spirit has made us all, but He has made a grea diff rence between His white and His red children. He has given us different complexions and different customs. To you He has given the arts. To these He has not opened our eyes. We know these things to be true. Since He has made so great a difference between us in other things, why may we not conclude that He has given us a different religion according to our understanding? The Great Spirit does right. He knows what is best for His children; we are satisfied.

Brother, we do not wish to destroy your religion or take it from you. We only want to enjoy our own.

Brother, you say you have not come to get our land or our money, but to enlighten our minds. I will now tell you that I have been at your meetings and saw you collect money from the meeting. I can not tell what this money was intended for, but suppose that it was for your minister; and, if we should conform to your way of thinking, perhaps you may want some from us.

Brother, we are told that you have been preaching to the white people in this place. These people are our neighbors. We are acquainted with them. We will wait a little while and see what effect your preaching has upon them. If we find it does them good, makes them honest, and less disposed to cheat Indians, we will then consider again of what you have said.

Brother, you have now heard our answer to your talk, and this is all we have to say at present. As we are going to part, we will come and take you by the hand, and hope the Great Spirit will protect you on your journey and return you safe to your friends.

IV

TECUMSEH TO GOVERNOR HARRISON AT VINCENNES [1]

(1810)

Born about 1768, died in 1813; a Chief of the Shawnee and twin
brother of Elskwatawa, who was defeated by Harrison at Tippe-
canoe; joined the British in the War of 1812; fought in several battles in Canada; commanded the right wing of the allied Indian and
British forces, who were defeated in the Battle of the Thames by
General Harrison.

It is true I am a Shawnee. My forefathers
were warriors. Their son is a warrior. From
them I take only my existence; from my tribe
I take nothing. I am the maker of my own
fortune; and oh! that I could make that of my
red people, and of my country, as great as the
conceptions of my mind, when I think of the
Spirit that rules the universe. I would not
then come to Governor Harrison to ask him to
tear the treaty and to obliterate the landmark;
but I would say to him: "Sir, you have liberty to
return to your own country."

The being within, communing with past ages,
tells me that once, nor until lately, there was no
white man on this continent; that it then all be-
longed to red men, children of the same parents,

[1] Delivered to Governor Harrison in council at Vincennes on
August 12, 1810. Large tracts of land in Tecumseh's absence had
been sold by the Indians on both sides of the Wabash River.

placed on it by the Great Spirit that made them, to keep it, to traverse it, to enjoy its productions, and to fill it with the same race, once a happy race, since made miserable by the white people, who are never contented but always encroaching. The way, and the only way, to check and to stop this evil, is for all the red men to unite in claiming a common and equal right in the land, as it was at first, and should be yet; for it never was divided, but belongs to all for the use of each. For no part has a right to sell, even to each other, much less to strangers— those who want all, and will not do with less.

The white people have no right to take the land from the Indians, because they had it first; it is theirs. They may sell, but all must join. Any sale not made by all is not valid. The late sale is bad. It was made by a part only. Part do not know how to sell. It requires all to make a bargain for all. All red men have equal rights to the unoccupied land. The right of occupancy is as good in one place as in another. There can not be two occupations in the same place. The first excludes all others. It is not so in hunting or traveling; for there the same ground will serve many, as they may follow each other all day; but the camp is stationary, and that is occupancy. It belongs to the first who sits down on his blanket or skins which he has thrown upon the ground; and till he leaves it no other has a right.

V

TECUMSEH TO GENERAL PROCTOR [1]
(1813)

FATHER, listen to your children! you have them now all before you. The war before this, our British father gave the hatchet to his red children when old chiefs were alive. They are now dead. In that war our father was thrown on his back by the Americans, and our father took them by the hand without our knowledge; and we are afraid that our father will do so again at this time.

Summer before last, when I came forward with my red brethren and was ready to take up the hatchet in favor of our British father, we were told not to be in a hurry; that he had not yet determined to fight the Americans.

Listen! When war was declared, our father stood up and gave us the tomahawk, and told us that he was ready to strike the Americans; that he wanted our assistance, and that he would

[1] Delivered "in the name of the Indian chiefs and warriors to Major-General [Henry A.] Proctor, as the representative of their great father, the king," a short time before the Battle of the Thames in Canada, which occurred on October 5, 1813. Proctor, totally defeated by Gen. William Henry Harrison, was court-martialed and suspended from his rank and pay, but reinstated afterward and rose to be a lieutenant-general. This speech was first published in 1813 in the *National Intelligencer* of Washington, with a note saying it was "found among General Proctor's papers after his flight."

certainly get us our lands back, which the Americans had taken from us.

Listen! You told us at that time to bring forward our families to this place, and we did so; and you promised to take care of them, and that they should want for nothing while the men would go and fight the enemy. That we need not trouble ourselves about the enemy's garrisons; that we knew nothing about them, and that our father would attend to that part of the business. You also told your red children that you would take good care of your garrison here, which made our hearts glad.

Listen! When we were last at the Rapids, it is true we gave you little assistance. It is hard to fight people who live like ground-hogs.

Father, listen! Our fleet has gone out; we know they have fought; we have heard the great guns, but know nothing of what has happened to our father with one arm. Our ships have gone one way, and we are much astonished to see our father tying up everything and preparing to run away the other, without letting his red children know what his intentions are. You always told us to remain here and take care of our lands. It made our hearts glad to hear that was your wish. Our great father, the king, is the head, and you represent him. You always told us that you would never draw your foot off British ground; but now, father, we see you are drawing back, and we are sorry to see our father doing so without seeing the enemy. We must compare our father's conduct to a fat animal that carries its tail upon its back, but when affrighted it drops it between its legs and runs off.

Listen, father! The Americans have not yet defeated us by land; neither are we sure that they have done so by water; we therefore wish to remain here and fight our enemy should they make their appearance. If they defeat us, we will then retreat with our father.

At the Battle of the Rapids, last war, the Americans certainly defeated us; and when we retreated to our father's fort in that place the gates were shut against us. We were afraid that it would now be the case, but instead of that we now see our British father preparing to march out of his garrison.

Father! You have got the arms and ammunition which our great father sent for his red children. If you have an idea of going away, give them to us, and you may go and welcome; for us, our lives are in the hands of the Great Spirit. We are determined to defend our lands, and if it is His will we wish to leave our bones upon them.

VI

PUSHMATAHA TO JOHN C. CALHOUN [1]
(1824)

Born in 1765, died in 1824; a Chief of the Choctaws; had a notable career as a Warrior against the Osage Indians and in Mexico; served with the Americans in the War of 1812.

FATHER, I have been here at the council-house for some time, but I have not talked. I have not been strong enough to talk. You shall hear me talk to-day. I belong to another district. You have, no doubt, heard of me. I am Pushmataha.

Father, when in my own country, I often looked toward this council-house, and wanted to come here. I am in trouble. I will tell my distresses. I feel like a small child, not half as

---

[1] Pushmataha's name is sometimes spelled Pushmatahaw, the word meaning "The warrior's seat is finished." In 1824 he went to Washington "to brighten the chain of peace," where he was treated with great attention by President Monroe and John C. Calhoun, then secretary of war, to whom he made the speech here given, a copy being now preserved in the official records of the War Department. Soon afterward he died. One of his last requests was that he might be buried with military honors. The procession that followed his body to the Congressional Cemetery was estimated to be more than a mile in length, the sidewalks, stoops and windows of houses being thronged along the way, and minute guns being fired from the hill of the capitol. John Randolph, in a eulogy pronounced in the Senate, characterized him as "one of nature's nobility; a man who would have adorned any society." On his tombstone he is described as "a warrior of great distinction; he was wise in counsel, eloquent in an extraordinary degree, and, on all occasions and under all circumstances, the white man's friend." Andrew

high as its father, who comes up to look in his
father's face, hanging in the bend of his arm,
to tell him his troubles. So, father, I hang in
the bend of your arm, and look in your face;
and now hear me speak.

Father, when I was in my own country, I
heard there were men appointed to talk to us.
I would not speak there; I chose to come here,
and speak in this beloved house; for Pushmataha can boast and say, and tell the truth, that
none of his fathers, or grandfathers, or any
Choctaw,[1] ever drew bow against the United

Jackson said he was "the greatest and the bravest Indian he had
ever known." During a visit to Lafayette, who was then in Washington, Pushmataha, being accompanied by other Indians of his
tribe, made the following speech:

"Nearly fifty snows have melted since you drew your sword as a
companion of Washington. With him you fought the enemies of
America. You mingled your blood with that of the enemy, and
proved yourself a warrior. After you finished that war, you returned to your own country, and now you are come back to revisit
the land where you are honored by a numerous and powerful people. You see everywhere the children of those by whose side you
went to battle crowding around you and shaking your hand as the
hand of a father. We have heard these things told in our distant
villages, and our hearts longed to see you. We have come; we have
taken you by the hand and are satisfied. This is the first time we
have seen you; it will probably be the last. We have no more to
say. The earth will part us for ever."

Pushmataha was taken ill just after this visit to Lafayette. On
his death-bed he said to his Indian companions: "When you shall
come to your home they will ask you, 'Where is Pushmataha?'
and you will say to them: 'He is no more!' They will hear the
tidings like the sound of the fall of a mighty oak in the stillness of
the woods."

[1] The Choctaws had formerly lived in southern Alabama and Mississippi, but after the Revolution they began to drift westward. In
1830 the last remnant had departed, their lands east of the Mississippi River being in that year ceded to the whites.

States. They have always been friendly. We have held the hands of the United States so long that our nails are long like birds' claws; and there is no danger of their slipping out.

Father, I have come to speak. My nation has always listened to the applications of the white people. They have given of their country till it is very small. I came here, when a young man, to see my Father Jefferson. He told me, if ever we got in trouble, we must run and tell him. I am come. This is a friendly talk; it is like that of a man who meets another, and says: "How do you do?" Another of my tribe shall talk further. He shall say what Pushmataha would say, were he stronger.

VII

BLACK HAWK TO GENERAL STREET[1]
(1832)

Born in 1767, died in 1838; succeeded his father as Chief of the Sac Indians in 1788; acted against the Americans in the War of 1812; because of the occupation by the whites of certain vacated lands, began the Black Hawk War in 1831; defeated in two battles in 1832; surrendered, taken East and confined in Fortress Monroe until June, 1833.

You have taken me prisoner, with all my warriors. I am much grieved; for I expected, if I did not defeat you, to hold out much longer, and give you more trouble, before I surrendered. I tried hard to bring you into ambush, but your last general understood Indian fighting. I determined to rush on you, and fight you face to face. I fought hard. But your

[1] Delivered in the late summer of 1832. General Street appears to have been a militia officer. Black Hawk, having been defeated in July and August by General Dodge and General Atkinson in battles on the Wisconsin and Bad Axe Rivers, made his surrender to Street at Prairie du Chien on August 27, and was placed in the immediate charge of a young lieutenant, Jefferson Davis, afterward president of the Southern Confederacy. It is curious that Robert Anderson, who commanded at Fort Sumter, and Abraham Lincoln were serving at this time against Black Hawk; and, curious again, that Black Hawk, on being taken to the East a captive, was confined in Fortress Monroe, where, thirty-three years afterward, Jefferson Davis was confined. Before going to Fortress Monroe, Black Hawk was taken to Washington and presented to Andrew Jackson in the White House, where he saluted him in words which then could not have raised the smile which they raise now: "I am a man and you are another."

guns were well aimed. The bullets flew like birds in the air, and whizzed by our ears like the wind through the trees in winter. My warriors fell around me; it began to look dismal.

I saw my evil day at hand. The sun rose dim on us in the morning, and at night it sank in a dark cloud, and looked like a ball of fire. That was the last sun that shone on Black Hawk. His heart is dead, and no longer beats quick in his bosom. He is now a prisoner of the white men; they will do with him as they wish. But he can stand torture, and is not afraid of death. He is no coward. Black Hawk is an Indian. He has done nothing for which an Indian ought to be ashamed. He has fought for his countrymen, against white men, who came, year after year, to cheat them and take away their lands.

You know the cause of our making war. It is known to all white men. They ought to be ashamed of it. The white men despise the Indians, and drive them from their homes. They smile in the face of the poor Indian, to cheat him; they shake him by the hand, to gain his confidence, to make him drunk, and to deceive him. We told them to let us alone, and keep away from us; but they followed on and beset our paths, and they coiled themselves among us like the snake. They poisoned us by their touch. We were not safe. We lived in danger. We looked up to the Great Spirit. We went to our father. We were encouraged. His great council gave us fair words and big promises, but we got no satisfaction: things were growing worse. There were no deer in the forest. The opossum and beaver were fled. The springs were drying up, and our squaws and papooses were without food to keep them from starving.

We called a great council and built a large fire. The spirit of our fathers arose, and spoke to us to avenge our wrongs or die. We set up the war-whoop, and dug up the tomahawk; our knives were ready, and the heart of Black Hawk swelled high in his bosom, when he led his warriors to battle. He is satisfied. He will go to the world of spirits contented. He has done his duty. His father will meet him there, and commend him.

Black Hawk is a true Indian, and disdains to cry like a woman. He feels for his wife, his children, and his friends. But he does not care for himself. He cares for the Nation and the Indians. They will suffer. He laments their fate. Farewell, my Nation! Black Hawk tried to save you, and avenge your wrongs. He drank the blood of some of the whites. He has been taken prisoner, and his plans are crushed. He can do no more. He is near his end. His sun is setting, and he will rise no more. Farewell to Black Hawk!

VIII

PETER WILSON ON THE EMPIRE STATE[1]
(1847)

You see before you an Iroquois; yes, a native American! You have heard the history of the Indian trails and the geography of the State of New York before it was known to the palefaces. The land of Ga-nun-no[2] was once laced by these trails from Albany to Buffalo, trails that my people had trod for centuries—worn so deep by the feet of the Iroquois that they became your own roads of travel, when my people no longer walked in them. Your highways still lie in those paths; the same lines of communication bind one part of the Long House to another. My friend has told you that the Iroquois have no monuments. These highways are their monuments; this land of Ga-nun-no, this Empire State, is our monument. We wish to lay our bones under its soil, among those of our fathers. We shall not long occupy much room in living—still less when we are gone.

Have we, the first holders of this prosperous region, no longer a share in that history? Glad

[1] Delivered before the New York Historical Society on May 4, 1847. Peter Wilson was a Cayuga chief, whose Indian name, Waowawanaonk, means, "They hear his voice." Printed here from a copy in the archives of the Society. Abridged.

[2] A name by which the Indians have known the State of New York.

were your forefathers to sit down upon the threshhold of the Long House. Rich did they then hold themselves in getting the mere sweepings from its door. Had our forefathers spurned you from it, when the French were thundering at the opposite end to cut a passage through and drive you into the sea, whatever has been the fate of other Indians, the Iroquois might still have been a nation; and I, too, might have had—a country!

There was a prophet of our race in early times who said that the day would come when troubles would fall upon the Indians so that they would knock their heads together. When that time came they were to search for a large palm-tree and shelter their heads beneath its shade, letting their bodies be buried at its roots, and cause that tree to flourish and become a fitting monument of the Iroquois race. That time has now come; we are in trouble and distress—we knock our heads together in agony, and we desire to find the palm-tree that we may lie down and die beneath it. We wish that palm-tree to be the State of New York, that it may be the monument of the Iroquois.

JAMES OTIS

IN OPPOSITION TO WRITS OF ASSIST-
ANCE [1]

(1761)

Born in 1725, died in 1783; a Law Officer under the Crown; Member of the Massachusetts House of Representatives; Delegate to the Stamp Act Congress in 1765; wrote a pamphlet entitled, "Rights of the British Colonies Asserted," in 1764, and others that attracted wide attention in England as well as here; owing to illness, not active during the war; killed by lightning in 1783.

MAY it please your honors, I was desired by one of the court to look into the books, and consider the question now before them concerning writs of assistance. I have, accordingly, considered it, and now appear not only in obedience to your order, but likewise in behalf of the inhabitants of this town, who have presented another petition, and out of regard to the liberties of the subject. And I take this opportunity to declare that, whether under a fee or not (for in such a cause as this I despise a fee), I will to my dying day oppose with all the powers and faculties God has given me all such instruments of slavery on the one hand, and villainy on the other, as this writ of assistance is.

[1] Delivered before the Superior Court in Boston in February, 1761, and the earliest important word publicly uttered in the controversies which precipitated the Revolution. John Adams declared that in this oration "American independence was born." Abridged.

It appears to me the worst instrument of arbitrary power, the most destructive of English liberty and the fundamental principles of law, that ever was found in an English law book. I must, therefore, beg your honors' patience and attention to the whole range of argument that may, perhaps, appear uncommon in many things, as well as to points of learning that are more remote and unusual; that the whole tendency of my design may the more easily be perceived, the conclusions better descend, and the force of them be better felt.

I shall not think much of my pains in this cause, as I engaged in it from principle. I was solicited to argue this cause as advocate-general; and because I would not, I have been charged with desertion from my office. To this charge I can give a very sufficient answer. I renounced that office, and I argue this cause from the same principle; and I argue it with the greater pleasure, as it is in favor of British liberty, at a time when we hear the greatest monarch upon earth declaring from his throne that he glories in the name of Briton, and that the privileges of his people are dearer to him than the most valuable prerogatives of his crown; and as it is in opposition to a kind of power, the exercise of which, in former periods of history, cost one king of England his head and another his throne. I have taken more pains in this cause than I ever will take again, altho my engaging in this and another popular cause has raised much resentment. But I think I can sincerely declare that I cheerfully submit myself to every odious name for conscience' sake; and from my soul I despise all those whose guilt, malice, or folly has made them my foes. Let the consequences be what they will, I am determined to proceed. The only principles of public conduct that are worthy of a gentleman or a man are to sacrifice estate, ease, health, and applause, and even life, to the sacred calls of his country.

These manly sentiments, in private life, make the good citizen; in public life, the patriot and the hero. I do not say that when brought to the test, I shall be invincible. I pray God I may never be brought to the melancholy trial; but if ever I should, it will be then known how far I can reduce to practise principles which I know to be founded in truth. In the meantime I will proceed to the subject of this writ.

Your honors will find in the old books concerning the office of a justice of the peace precedents of general warrants to search suspected houses. But in more modern books, you will find only special warrants to search such and such houses, specially named, in which the complainant has before sworn that he suspects his goods are concealed; and will find it adjudged that special warrants only are legal. In the same manner I rely on it, that the writ prayed for in this petition, being general, is illegal. It is a power that places the liberty of every man in the hands of every petty officer. I say I admit that special writs of assistance, to search special places, may be granted to certain persons on oath; but I deny that the writ now prayed for can be granted, for I beg leave to make some observations on the writ itself, before I proceed to other Acts of Parliament.

In the first place, the writ is universal, being directed "to all and singular justices, sheriffs, constables, and all other officers and subjects"; so that, in short, it is directed to every subject in the king's dominions. Every one with this writ may be a tyrant; if this commission be legal, a tyrant in a legal manner, also, may control, imprison, or murder any one within the realm.

In the next place, it is perpetual; there is no return. A man is accountable to no person for his doings. Every man may reign secure in his petty tyranny, and spread terror and desolation around him, until the trump of the archangel shall excite different emotions in his soul.

In the third place, a person with this writ, in the daytime, may enter all houses, shops, etc., at will, and command all to assist him.

Fourthly, by this writ, not only deputies, etc., but even their menial servants, are allowed to lord it over us. What is this but to have the curse of Canaan with a witness on us; to be the servant of servants, the most despicable of God's creation?

Now one of the most essential branches of English liberty is the freedom of one's house.

A man's house is his castle; and while he is quiet, he is as well guarded as a prince in his castle. This writ, if it should be declared legal, would totally annihilate this privilege. Customhouse officers may enter our houses when they please; we are commanded to permit their entry. Their menial servants may enter, may break locks, bars, and everything in their way; and whether they break through malice or revenge, no man, no court can inquire. Bare suspicion without oath is sufficient. This wanton exercise of this power is not a chimerical suggestion of a heated brain.

I will mention some facts. Mr. Pew had one of these writs, and when Mr. Ware succeeded him, he indorsed this writ over to Mr. Ware; so that these writs are negotiable from one officer to another, and so your honors have no opportunity of judging the persons to whom this vast power is delegated. Another instance is this: Mr. Justice Walley had called this same Mr. Ware before him, by a constable, to answer for a breach of the Sabbath Day Acts, or that of profane swearing. As soon as he had finished, Mr. Ware asked him if he had done. He replied: "Yes." "Well, then," said Mr. Ware, "I will show you a little of my power. I command you to permit me to search your house for uncustomed goods"; and went on to search the house from the garret to the cellar, and then served the constable in the same manner! But to show another absurdity in this writ, if it should be established, I insist upon it that every person, by the 14th of Charles II., has this power as well as the custom-house officers. The words are: "It shall be lawful for any person or persons authorized," etc. What a scene does this open! Every man prompted by revenge, ill humor, or wantonness, to inspect the inside of his neighbor's house, may get a writ of assistance. Others will ask it from self-defense; one arbitrary exertion will provoke another, until society be involved in tumult and in blood.[1]

2. "He asserted that every man, merely natural, was an independent sovereign, subject to no law but the law written on his heart and revealed to him by his Maker, in the constitution of his nature, and the inspiration of his understanding and his conscience. His right to his life, his liberty, no created being could rightfully contest. Nor was his right to his property less incontestible. The club that he had snapped from a tree, for a staff or for defense, was his own. His bow and arrow were his own; if by a pebble he had killed a partridge or a squirrel, it was his own. No creature, man or beast, had a right to take it from him. If he had taken an eel, or a smelt, or a sculpin, it was his property. In short, he sported upon this topic with so much wit and humor, and at the same time with so much indisputable truth and reason, that he was

---

[1] Of this famous speech by Otis, we have no report beyond this point except in the account which John Adams wrote down in the third person, as given in the paragraphs which follow.

not less entertaining than instructive. He asserted that these rights were inherent and inalienable; that they never could be surrendered or alienated, but by idiots or madmen, and all the acts of idiots and lunatics were void, and not obligatory, by all the laws of God and man. Nor were the poor negroes forgotten. Not a Quaker in Philadelphia, or Mr. Jefferson in Virginia, ever asserted the rights of negroes in stronger terms. Young as I was, and ignorant as I was, I shuddered at the doctrine he taught; and I have all my life shuddered, and still shudder, at the consequences that may be drawn from such premises. Shall we say that the rights of masters and servants clash, and can be decided only by force? I adore the idea of gradual abolitions! but who shall decide how fast or how slowly these abolitions shall be made?

3. "From individual independence he proceeded to association. If it was inconsistent with the dignity of human nature to say that men were gregarious animals, like wild geese, it surely could offend no delicacy to say they were social animals by nature; that there were natural sympathies, and, above all, the sweet attraction of the sexes, which must soon draw them together in little groups, and by degrees in larger congregations, for mutual assistance and defense. And this must have happened before any formal covenant, by express words or signs, was concluded. When general councils and deliberations commenced, the objects could be no other than the

mutual defense and security of every individual
for his life, his liberty, and his property. To
suppose them to have surrendered these in any
other way than by equal rules and general consent was to suppose them idiots or madmen,
whose acts were never binding. To suppose
them surprised by fraud, or compelled by force
into any other compact, such fraud and such
force could confer no obligation. Every man
had a right to trample it under foot whenever he
pleased. In short, he asserted these rights to be
derived only from nature and the Author of
nature; that they were inherent, inalienable, and
indefeasible by any laws, pacts, contracts, cove-
nants, or stipulations which man could devise.

4. "These principles and these rights were
wrought into the English Constitution as fundamental laws. And under this head he went back
to the old Saxon laws, and to Magna Charta, and
the fifty confirmations of it in Parliament, and
the executions ordained against the violators of it,
and the national vengeance which had been taken
on them from time to time, down to the Jameses
and Charleses, and to the Petition of Right and
the Bill of Rights and the Revolution. He asserted that the security of these rights to life,
liberty, and property had been the object of all
those struggles against arbitrary power, temporal
and spiritual, civil and political, military and
ecclesiastical, in every age. He asserted that our
ancestors, as British subjects, and we, their descendants, as British subjects, were entitled to

all those rights, by the British Constitution, as well as by the law of nature and our provincial charter, as much as any inhabitant of London or Bristol, or any part of England; and were not to be cheated out of them by any phantom of 'virtual representation,' or any other fiction of law or politics, or any monkish trick of deceit and hypocrisy.

5. ''He then examined the Acts of Trade, one by one, and demonstrated that if they were considered as revenue laws, they destroyed all our security of property, liberty, and life, every right of nature, and the English Constitution, and the charter of the province. Here he considered the distinction between 'external and internal taxes,' at that time a popular and commonplace distinction. But he asserted that there was no such distinction in theory, or upon any principle but 'necessity.' The necessity that the commerce of the Empire should be under one direction was obvious. The Americans had been so sensible of this necessity that they had connived at the distinction between external and internal taxes, and had submitted to the Acts of Trade as regulations of commerce, but never as taxations or revenue laws. Nor had the British government till now ever dared to attempt to enforce them as taxations or revenue laws. They had lain dormant in that character for a century almost. The Navigation Act he allowed to be binding upon us, because we had consented to it by our own legislature. Here he gave a history of

the Navigation Act of the 1st of Charles II., a plagiarism from Oliver Cromwell. This act had lain dormant for fifteen years. In 1675, after repeated letters and orders from the king, Governor Leverett very candidly informs his majesty that the law had not been executed, because it was thought unconstitutional, Parliament not having authority over us."

FRANKLIN

I

HIS EXAMINATION BEFORE THE HOUSE OF COMMONS[1]

(1766)

Born in Boston in 1706, died in 1790; settled in Philadelphia in 1729; Postmaster of Philadelphia in 1737; discovered the identity of lightning with electricity in 1753; proposed a "Plan of Union" at Albany in 1754; Colonial Agent for Pennsylvania in England, 1757-62 and 1764-75; Member of the Second Continental Congress in 1775; Member of the Committee which drew up the Declaration of Independence in 1776; Ambassador to France in 1776; helped to negotiate the treaty of peace with France in 1778; helped to negotiate the treaty of peace with England in 1783; President of Pennsylvania 1785-88; Member of the Constitutional Convention in 1787.

Q. ARE not the Colonies, from their circumstances, very able to pay the stamp duty?

A. In my opinion there is not gold and silver enough in the Colonies to pay the stamp duty for one year.

Q. Do you not know that the money arising from the stamps was all to be laid out in America?

A. I know it is appropriated by the Act to the American service; but it will be spent in

[1] First published in London in 1766 as "The Examination of Doctor Franklin." Owing to the secrecy of the session of Parliament no clue was given in the pamphlet as to the place where the examination had been held, nor as to where or by whom the pamphlet was printed. J. Almon, who caused it to be printed, feared prosecution, but none having been begun, he next year printed the examination as having taken place " before an honorable assembly relative to

37

the conquered Colonies, where the soldiers are; not in the Colonies that pay it.

Q. Do you think it right that America should be protected by this country and pay no part of the expense?

A. That is not the case. The Colonies raised, clothed, and paid, during the last war, near twenty-five thousand men, and spent many millions.

Q. Were you not reimbursed by Parliament?

A. We were only reimbursed what, in your opinion, we had advanced beyond our proportion, or beyond what might reasonably be expected from us; and it was a very small part of what we spent. Pennsylvania, in particular, disbursed about £500,000, and the reimbursements, in the whole, did not exceed £60,000.

Q. Do you not think the people of America would submit to pay the stamp duty if it was moderated?

A. No, never, unless compelled by force of arms.

Q. What was the temper of America toward Great Britain *before the year* 1763?

A. The best in the world. They submitted willingly to the government of the Crown, and

the repeal of the American Stamp Act in 1776." A still later edition described the examination as having taken place "before an august assembly." The pamphlet was reprinted in 1766 in several American cities, including Philadelphia, New York, Boston, and New London. In Pennsylvania it was said that the demand for it "from all parts of the province was beyond conception."

It has been often stated that many of the questions propounded paid, in their courts, obedience to acts of Parliament. Numerous as the people are in the several old provinces they cost you nothing in forts, citadels, garrisons, or armies, to keep them in subjection. They were governed by this country at the expense only of a little pen, ink, and paper; they were led by a thread. They had not only a respect but an affection for Great Britain; for its laws, its customs, and manners, and even a fondness for its fashions, that greatly increased the commerce. Natives of Britain were always treated with particular regard; to be an *Old England-man* was of itself a character of some respect, and gave a kind of rank among us.

Q. And what is their temper now?

A. Oh, very much altered!

Q. Did you ever hear the authority of Parliament to make laws for America questioned till lately?

A. The authority of Parliament was allowed to be valid in all laws, except such as should lay internal taxes. It was never disputed in laying duties to regulate commerce.

Q. In what light did the people of America use to consider the Parliament of Great Britain?

to Franklin had already been skilfully arranged for between Franklin and the enemies of the Stamp Act. But John T. Morse, one of Franklin's biographers, says: "It does not appear that such prearrangements went further than that certain friendly interrogators had discussed the topics with him, so as to be familiar with his views. Every lawyer does this with his witnesses. Nor can it be supposed that the admirable replies which he made

A. They considered the Parliament as the great bulwark and security of their liberties and privileges, and always spoke of it with the utmost respect and veneration. Arbitrary ministers, they thought, might possibly, at times, attempt to oppress them; but they relied on it, that the Parliament, on application, would always give redress. They remembered, with gratitude, a strong instance of this, when a bill was brought into Parliament with a clause to make royal instructions laws in the Colonies which the House of Commons would not pass, and it was thrown out.

Q. And have they not still the same respect for Parliament?

A. No; it is greatly lessened.

Q. To what causes is that owing?

A. To a concurrence of causes: the restraints lately laid on their trade, by which the bringing of foreign gold and silver into the Colonies was prevented; the prohibition of making paper money among themselves, and then demanding a new and heavy tax by stamps; taking away, at the same time, trials by juries, and refusing to receive and hear their humble petitions.

Q. Do you not think they would submit to the

to the enemies of America were otherwise than strictly impromptu." Burke likened the proceedings to "an examination of a master, by a parcel of schoolboys." Franklin afterward said that the friends of the repeal "were ready to hug me for the assistance that I afforded them." Among those that asked questions were Grenville, Townshend, North, Thurlow, and Burke. The examination closed on February 15, 1766. Abridged.

Stamp Act if it was modified, the obnoxious parts taken out, and the duty reduced to some particulars of small moment?

A. No; they will never submit to it.

Q. Was it an opinion in America before 1763 that the Parliament had no right to lay taxes and duties there?

A. I never heard an objection to the right of laying duties to regulate commerce; but a right to lay internal taxes was never supposed to be in Parliament, as we are not represented there.

Q. On what do you found your opinion that the people in America made any such distinction?

A. I know that whenever the subject has occurred in conversation where I have been present, it has appeared to be the opinion of every one that we could not be taxed by a Parliament wherein we were not represented. But the payment of duties laid by an act of Parliament as regulations of commerce was never disputed.

Q. But can you name any act of assembly or public act of any of your governments that made such distinction?

A. I do not know that there was any. I think there was never an occasion to make any such act till now that you have attempted to tax us; *that* has occasioned resolutions of assembly declaring the distinction, in which I think every assembly on the continent and every member in every assembly have been unanimous.

Q. You say the Colonies have always submitted to external taxes, and object to the right of Parliament only in laying internal taxes; now can you show that there is any kind of *difference between the two taxes* to the Colony on which they may be laid?

A. I think the difference is very great. An *external* tax is a duty laid on commodities imported; that duty is added to the first cost and other charges on the commodity, and, when it is offered for sale, makes a part of the price. If the people do not like it at that price, they refuse it; they are not obliged to pay it. But an *internal* tax is forced from the people without their consent if not laid by their own representatives. The Stamp Act says we shall have no commerce, make no exchange of property with each other, neither purchase nor grant, nor recover debts; we shall neither marry nor make our wills, unless we pay such and such sums; and thus it is intended to extort our money from us or ruin us by the consequence of refusing to pay it.

Q. But supposing the external tax or duty to be laid on the necessaries of life imported into your Colony; will not that be the same thing in its effects as an internal tax?

A. I do not know a single article imported into the *northern* Colonies but what they can either do without or make themselves.

Q. Do you not think cloth from England absolutely necessary to them?

A. No, by no means absolutely necessary; with industry and good management, they may very well supply themselves with all they want.

Q. Will it not take a long time to establish that manufacture among them; and must they not, in the meanwhile, suffer greatly?

A. I think not. They have made a surprising progress already. And I am of the opinion that before their old clothes are worn out they will have new ones of their own making.

Q. Can they possibly find wool enough in North America?

A. They have taken steps to increase the wool. They entered into general combinations to eat no more lamb, and very few lambs were killed last year. This course persisted in will soon make a prodigious difference in the quantity of wool. And the establishment of great manufactories, like those in the clothing towns here, is not necessary as it is where the business is to be carried on for the purposes of trade. The people will all spin and work for themselves in their own houses.

Q. Considering the resolutions of Parliament, *as to the right;* do you think if the Stamp Act is repealed that the North Americans will be satisfied?

A. I believe they will.

Q. Why do you think so?

A. I think the resolutions of *right* will give them very little concern if they are never attempted to be carried into practise. The Colonies will probably consider themselves in the same situation in that respect with Ireland; they know you claim the same right with regard to Ireland, but you never exercise it. And they may believe you never will exercise it in the Colonies any more than in Ireland, unless on some very extraordinary occasion.

Q. But who are to be the judges of that extraordinary occasion? Is not the Parliament?

A. Tho the Parliament may judge of the occasion, the people will think it can never exercise such right till representatives from the Colonies are admitted into Parliament; and that, whenever the occasion arises, representatives *will* be ordered.

Q. Can anything less than a military force carry the Stamp Act into execution?

A. I do not see how a military force can be applied to that purpose.

Q. Why may it not?

A. Suppose a military force sent into America: they will find nobody in arms; what are they then to do? They can not force a man to take stamps who chooses to do without them. They will not find a rebellion; they may, indeed, make one.

Q. If the Act is not repealed, what do you think will be the consequences?

A. A total loss of the respect and affection the people of America bear to this country, and of all the commerce that depends on that respect and affection.

Q. How can the commerce be affected?

A. You will find that if the Act is not repealed they will take very little of your manufactures in a short time.

Q. Is it in their power to do without them?

A. I think they may very well do without them.

Q. Is it to their interest not to take them?

A. The goods they take from Britain are either necessaries, mere conveniences, or superfluities. The first, as cloth, etc., with a little industry, they can make at home; the second they can do without till they are able to provide them among themselves; and the last, which are much the greatest part, they will strike off immediately. They are mere articles of fashion, purchased and consumed because the fashion in a respected country, but will now be detested and rejected. The people have already struck off, by general agreement, the use of all goods fashionable in mourning, and many thousand pounds' worth are sent back as unsalable.

Q. Then no regulation with a tax would be submitted to?

A. Their opinion is that when aids to the Crown are wanted they are to be asked of the several assemblies according to the old-established usage, who will, as they always have done, grant them freely, and that their money ought not to be given away without their consent, by persons at a distance, unacquainted with their circumstances and abilities. The

granting aids to the Crown is the only means
they have of recommending themselves to their
sovereign, and they think it extremely hard
and unjust that a body of men in which they
have no representatives should make a merit to
itself of giving and granting what is not its
own but theirs, and deprive them of a right
they esteem of the utmost value and importance,
as it is the security of all their other rights.

Q. Supposing the Stamp Act continued and
enforced, do you imagine that ill humor will induce the Americans to give as much for worse
manufactures of their own, and use them, pref-
erable to better of ours?

A. Yes, I think so. People will pay as freely to gratify one passion as another—their resentment as their pride.

Q. If the Stamp Act should be repealed,
would not the Americans think they could oblige
the Parliament to repeal every external tax-law
now in force?

A. It is hard to answer questions of what
people at such a distance will think.

Q. But what do you imagine they will think
were the motives of repealing the Act?

A. I suppose they will think that it was repealed from a conviction of its inexpediency;
and they will rely upon it that while the same
inexpediency subsists you will never attempt to
make such another.

Q. What do you mean by its inexpediency?

A. I mean its inexpediency on several accounts: the poverty and inability of those who were to pay the tax, the general discontent it has occasioned, and the impracticability of enforcing it.

Q. But if the legislature should think fit to ascertain its right to lay taxes by any act laying a small tax, contrary to their opinion, would they submit to pay the tax?

A. The proceedings of the people in America have been considered too much together. The proceedings of the assemblies have been very different from those of the mobs, and should be distinguished as having no connection with each other. The *assemblies* have only peaceably resolved what they take to be their rights; they have taken no measures for opposition by force, they have not built a fort, raised a man, or provided a grain of ammunition, in order to such opposition. The ringleaders of riots, they think, ought to be punished; they would punish them themselves if they could. Every sober, sensible man would wish to see rioters punished, as otherwise peaceable people have no security of person or estate; but as to an internal tax, how small soever, laid by the legislature here on the people there, while they have no representatives in this legislature, I think it will never be submitted to; they will oppose it to the last; they do not consider it as at all necessary for you to raise money on them by your taxes, because they are, and always have been, ready to raise money by taxes among themselves and to grant large sums, equal to their abilities, upon requisition from the Crown. They have not only granted equal to their abilities, but during all the last war they granted far beyond their abilities, and beyond their proportion with this country (you yourselves being judges) to the amount of many hundred thousand pounds; and this they did freely and readily, only on a sort of **promise** from the secretary of state that it should be recommended to Parliament to make them compensation. It was accordingly recommended to Parliament in the most honorable manner for them. America has been greatly misrepresented and abused here, in papers and pamphlets and speeches, . . . as ungrateful and **unreasonable** and unjust; in having put this nation to immense expense for their defense, and refusing to bear any part of that expense. The Colonies raised, paid, and clothed near twenty-five thousand men during the last war—a number equal to those sent from Britain, and far beyond their proportion; they went deeply into debt in doing this, and all their taxes and estates are mortgaged for many years to come for discharging that debt.

Q. But suppose Great Britain should be engaged in a *war in Europe*, would North America contribute to the support of it?

A. I do think they would, as far as their circumstances would permit. They consider themselves as a part of the British Empire, and as

having one common interest with it; they may
be looked on here as foreigners. but they do not
consider themselves as such. They are zealous
for the honor and prosperity of this nation,
and while they are well used will always be
ready to support it as far as their little
power goes. In 1739 they were called upon to
assist in the expedition against Cartagena, and
they sent three thousand men to join your
army. It is true Cartagena is in America, but
as remote from the northern Colonies as if it
had been in Europe. They make no distinction
of wars as to their duty of assisting in them.
I know the *last war* is commonly spoken of here
as entered into for the defense or for the sake
of the people in America. I think it is quite
misunderstood. It began about the limits between Canada and Nova Scotia, about territories to which the *Crown* indeed laid claim, but
which were not claimed by any British *Colony;*
none of the lands had been granted to any colo-
nist; we had, therefore, no particular interest
or concern in that dispute. As to the Ohio, the
contest there began about your right of trading
in the Indian country, a right you had by the
treaty of Utrecht, which the French infringed;
they seized the traders and their goods, which
were your manufactures; they took a fort which
a company of your merchants and their factors
and correspondents had erected there to secure
that trade. Braddock was sent with an army
to retake that fort (which was looked on here

as another encroachment on the king's territory) and to protect your trade. It was not till after his defeat that the Colonies were attacked. They were before in perfect peace with both French and Indians; the troops were not, therefore, sent for their defense. The trade with the Indians, tho carried on in America, is not an *American interest*. The people of America are chiefly farmers and planters; scarce anything that they raise or produce is an article of commerce with the Indians. The Indian trade is a *British interest;* it is carried on with British manufactures, for the profit of British merchants and manufacturers; therefore, the war, as it commenced for the defense of territories of the Crown (the property of no American) and for the defense of a trade purely British, was really a British war—and yet the people of America made no scruple of contributing their utmost toward carrying it on, and bringing it to a happy conclusion.

Q. Do you think the assemblies have a right to levy money on the subject there to grant *to the Crown?*

A. I certainly think so; they have always done it.

Q. Are they acquainted with the Declaration of Rights? And do they know that, by that Statute, money is not to be raised on the subject but by consent of Parliament?

A. They are very well acquainted with it.

Q. How, then, can they think they have a

right to levy money for the Crown or for any other than local purposes?

A. They understand that clause to relate to subjects only within the realm; that no money can be levied on them for the Crown but by consent of Parliament. *The Colonies* are not supposed to be within the realm; they have assemblies of their own, which are their parliaments, and they are, in that respect, in the same situation with Ireland. When money is to be raised for the Crown upon the subject in Ireland, or in the Colonies, the consent is given in the Parliament of Ireland or in the assemblies of the Colonies. They think the Parliament of Great Britain can not properly give that consent till it has representatives from America, for the Petition of Right expressly says it is to be by *common consent in Parliament*, and the people of America have no representatives in Parliament to make a part of that common consent.

Q. If the Stamp Act should be repealed, and the Crown should make a requisition to the Colonies for a sum of money, would they grant it?

A. I believe they would.

Q. Why do you think so?

A. I can speak for the Colony I live in. I had it in *instruction* from the Assembly to assure the ministry that as they always had done, so they should always think it their duty to grant such aids to the Crown as were suitable to their circumstances and abilities, whenever called upon for that purpose, in the usual constitutional manner; and I had the honor of communicating this instruction to that honorable gentleman then minister.

Q. Would they do this for a British concern, as suppose a war in some part of Europe, that did not affect them?

A. Yes; for anything that concerned the general interest. They consider themselves as part of the whole.

Q. If the Stamp Act should be repealed, would it induce the assemblies of America to acknowledge the rights of Parliament to tax them, and would they erase their resolutions?

A. No, never!

Q. Are there no means of obliging them to erase those resolutions?

A. None that I know of; they will never do it, unless compelled by force of arms.

Q. Is there a power on earth that can force them to erase them?

A. No power, how great soever, can force men to change their opinions.

Q. What used to be the pride of the Americans?

A. To indulge in the fashions and manufactures of Great Britain.

Q. What is now their pride?

A. To wear their old clothes over again till they can make new ones.

II

ON THE FEDERAL CONSTITUTION [1]
(1787)

I CONFESS that I do not entirely approve of this Constitution at present; but, sir, I am not sure I shall never approve of it, for, having lived long, I have experienced many instances of being obliged, by better information or fuller consideration, to change opinions even on important subjects, which I once thought right, but found to be otherwise. It is therefore that, the older I grow, the more apt I am to doubt my own judgment of others. Most men, indeed, as well as most sects in religion, think themselves in possession of all truth, and that wherever others differ from them, it is so far error. Steele, a Protestant, in a dedication, tells the pope that the only difference between our two churches in their opinions of the certainty of their doctrine is, the Romish Church is infallible, and the Church of England is never in the wrong. But, tho many private persons think almost as highly of their own infallibility as of that of their sect, few express it so naturally as a certain French lady, who, in a little dispute with her sister, said: "But I meet with nobody but myself that is always in the right."

[1] From a speech in Philadelphia before the Constitutional Convention of 1787.

In these sentiments, sir, I agree to this Constitution with all its faults—if they are such—because I think a general government necessary for us, and there is no form of government but what may be a blessing to the people if well administered; and I believe, further, that this is likely to be well administered for a course of years, and can only end in despotism, as other forms have done before it, when the people shall become so corrupted as to need despotic government, being incapable of any other. I doubt, too, whether any other convention we can obtain may be able to make a better Constitution; for, when you assemble a number of men, to have the advantage of their joint wisdom, you inevitably assemble with those men all their prejudices, their passions, their errors of opinion, their local interests, and their selfish views. From such an assembly can a perfect production be expected?

It therefore astonishes me, sir, to find this system approaching so near to perfection as it does; and I think it will astonish our enemies, who are waiting with confidence to hear that our counsels are confounded like those of the builders of Babel, and that our States are on the point of separation, only to meet hereafter for the purpose of cutting one another's throats. Thus I consent, sir, to this Constitution, because I expect no better, and because I am not sure that it is not the best. The opinions I have had of its errors I sacrifice to the public good. I

have never whispered a syllable of them abroad.
Within these walls they were born, and here
they shall die. If every one of us, in returning
to our constituents, were to report the objections he has had to it, and endeavor to gain
partizans in support of them, we might prevent
its being generally received, and thereby lose
all the salutary effects and great advantages resulting naturally in our favor among foreign nations, as well as among ourselves, from our real
or apparent unanimity. Much of the strength
and efficiency of any government, in procuring
and securing happiness to the people, depends on
opinion, on the general opinion of the goodness
of that government, as well as of the wisdom and
integrity of its governors. I hope, therefore, for
our own sakes, as a part of the people, and for
the sake of our posterity, that we shall act heart-
ily and unanimously in recommending this
Constitution wherever our influence may extend,
and turn our future thoughts and endeavors to
the means of having it well administered.

On the whole, sir, I can not help expressing a
wish that every member of the convention who
may still have objections to it, would, with me,
on this occasion, doubt a little of his own infallibility, and, to make manifest our unanimity, put
his name to this instrument.

III

DANGERS OF A SALARIED BUREAUCRACY [1]
(1787)

IT is with reluctance that I rise to express a disapprobation of any one article of the plan for which we are so much obliged to the honorable gentlemen who laid it before us. From its first reading I have borne a good will to it, and, in general, wished it success. In this particular of salaries to the executive branch, I happen to differ; and, as my opinion may appear new and chimerical, it is only from a persuasion that it is right, and from a sense of duty, that I hazard it. The committee will judge of my reasons when they have heard them, and their judgment may possibly change mine. I think I see inconveniences in the appointment of salaries; I see none in refusing them, but, on the contrary, great advantages.

Sir, there are two passions which have a powerful influence in the affairs of men. These are ambition and avarice—the love of power and the love of money. Separately, each of these has great force in prompting men to action; but, when united in view of the same object, they have, in many minds, the most violent effects. Place before the eyes of such men a post of honor, that shall, at the same time, be a place of profit,

---

[1] Delivered in Philadelphia in the Constitutional Convention of 1787.

and they will move heaven and earth to obtain it. The vast number of such places it is that renders the British government so tempestuous. The struggles for them are the true source of all those factions which are perpetually dividing the nation, distracting its councils, hurrying it sometimes into fruitless and mischievous wars, and often compelling a submission to dishonorable terms of peace.

And of what kind are the men that will strive for this profitable preeminence, through all the bustle of cabal, the heat of contention, the infinite mutual abuse of parties, tearing to pieces the best of characters? It will not be the wise and moderate, the lovers of peace and good order, the men fittest for the trust. It will be the bold and the violent, the men of strong passions and indefatigable activity in their selfish pursuits. These will thrust themselves into your government and be your rulers. And these, too, will be mistaken in the expected happiness of their situation, for their vanquished competitors, of the same spirit, and from the same motives, will perpetually be endeavoring to distress their administration, thwart their measures, and render them odious to the people.

Besides these evils, sir, tho we may set out in the beginning with moderate salaries, we shall find that such will not be of long continuance. Reasons will never be wanting for proposed augmentations; and there will always be a party for giving more to the rulers, that the rulers may be able, in return, to give more to them. Hence, as all history informs us, there has been in every state and kingdom a constant kind of warfare between the governing and the governed; the one striving to obtain more for its support, and the other to pay less. And this has alone occasioned great convulsions, actual civil wars, ending either in dethroning of the princes or enslaving of the people.

Generally, indeed, the ruling power carries its point, and we see the revenues of princes constantly increasing, and we see that they are never satisfied, but always in want of more. The more the people are discontented with the oppression of taxes, the greater need the prince has of money to distribute among his partizans, and pay the troops that are to suppress all resistance, and enable him to plunder at pleasure. There is scarce a king in a hundred who would not, if he could, follow the example of Pharaoh—get first all the people's money, then all their lands, and then make them and their children servants for ever. It will be said that we do not propose to establish kings. I know it. But there is a natural inclination in mankind to kingly government. It sometimes relieves them from aristocratic domination. They would rather have one tyrant than five hundred. It gives more of the appearance of equality among citizens; and that they like.

I am apprehensive, therefore—perhaps too apprehensive—that the government of the States may, in future times, end in a monarchy. But this catastrophe, I think, may be long delayed, if in our proposed system we do not sow the seeds of contention, faction, and tumult, by making our posts of honor places of profit. If we do, I fear that, tho we employ at first a number and not a single person, the number will, in time, be set aside; it will only nourish the fetus of a king (as the honorable gentleman from Virginia very aptly expressed it), and a king will the sooner be set over us.

It may be imagined by some that this is a Utopian idea, and that we can never find men to serve us in the executive department without paying them well for their services. I conceive this to be a mistake. Some existing facts present themselves to me which incline me to a contrary opinion. The high sheriff of a county in England is an honorable office, but it is not a profitable one. It is rather expensive, and therefore not sought for. But yet it is executed, and well executed, and usually by some of the principal gentlemen of the county. In France the office of counselor, or member of their judiciary parliament, is more honorable. It is therefore purchased at a high price; there are, indeed, fees on the law proceedings, which are divided among them, but these fees do not amount to more than three per cent. on the sum paid for the place. Therefore, as legal interest is there at five per cent., they, in fact, pay two per cent. for being allowed to do the judiciary business of the nation, which is, at the same time, entirely exempt from the burden of paying them any salaries for their services.

I do not, however, mean to recommend this as an eligible mode for our judiciary department. I only bring the instance to show that the pleasure of doing good and serving their country, and the respect such conduct entitles them to, are sufficient motives with some minds to give up a great portion of their time to the public, without the mean inducement of pecuniary satisfaction.

Another instance is that of a respectable society who have made the experiment and practised it with success now more than a hundred years. I mean the Quakers. It is an established rule with them that they are not to go to law, but in their controversies they must apply to their monthly, quarterly, and yearly meetings. Committees of these sit with patience to hear the parties, and spend much time in composing their differences. In doing this they are supported by a sense of duty and the respect paid to usefulness. It is honorable to be so employed, but it was never made profitable by salaries, fees, or perquisites. And, indeed, in all cases of public service, the less the profit, the greater the honor.

To bring the matter nearer home, have we not seen the greatest and most important of our offices, that of general of our armies, executed for eight years together, without the smallest salary, by a patriot whom I will not now offend by any other praise; and this, through fatigues and distresses, in common with the other brave men, his military friends and companions, and the constant anxieties peculiar to his station? And shall we doubt finding three or four men in all the United States with public spirit enough to bear sitting in peaceful council, for, perhaps, an equal term, merely to preside over our civil concerns, and see that our laws are duly executed? Sir, I have a better opinion of our country. I think we shall never be without a sufficient number of wise and good men to undertake and execute well and faithfully the office in question.

Sir, the saving of the salaries, that may at first be proposed, is not an object with me. The subsequent mischiefs of proposing them are what I apprehend. And, therefore, it is that I move the amendment. If it be not seconded or accepted, I must be contented with the satisfaction of having delivered my opinion frankly and done my duty.

PATRICK HENRY

I

THE "GIVE ME LIBERTY OR GIVE ME DEATH" SPEECH [1]

(1775)

Born in 1736, died in 1799; admitted to the Bar in 1760; entered the
Virginia House of Burgesses in 1765; acted with Thomas Jefferson
in promoting intercourse between the Colonies in 1773; Member of
the First Continental Congress in 1774; elected Governor of Virginia in 1776 and 1784; Member of the Convention which ratified the
Constitution in 1788, acting with the antifederalists.

No man thinks more highly than I do of the
patriotism, as well as abilities, of the very worthy
gentlemen who have just addressed the House.
But different men often see the same subject in
different lights; and, therefore, I hope it will not
be thought disrespectful to those gentlemen, if,
entertaining as I do opinions of a character very
opposite to theirs, I shall speak forth my sentiments freely and without reserve. This is no
time for ceremony.

The question before the House is one of awful

[1] Delivered on March 23, 1775, before the Second Revolutionary
Convention of Virginia, in the old church in Richmond. Of Patrick
Henry's famous "Treason" speech, made in the House of Burgesses in May, 1765, when he had introduced his resolutions against
the Stamp Act, only a fragment has come down to us. We are
told that in the midst of the debate he exclaimed, in a voice of
thunder and with the look of a god, "Cæsar had his Brutus, Charles

moment to this country. For my own part, I consider it as nothing less than a question of freedom or slavery; and in proportion to the magnitude of the subject ought to be the freedom of the debate. It is only in this way that we can hope to arrive at truth, and fulfil the great responsibility which we hold to God and our country. Should I keep back my opinions at such a time, through fear of giving offense, I should consider myself as guilty of treason toward my country, and of an act of disloyalty toward the Majesty of Heaven, which I revere above all earthly kings.

Mr. President, it is natural to man to indulge in the illusions of hope. We are apt to shut our eyes against a painful truth, and listen to the song of that siren, till she transforms us into beasts. Is this the part of wise men, engaged in a great and arduous struggle for liberty? Are we disposed to be of the number of those, who, having eyes, see not, and having ears, hear not, the things which so nearly concern their temporal salvation? For my part, whatever anguish of spirit it may cost, I am willing to know the whole truth; to know the worst, and to provide for it.

I have but one lamp by which my feet are

the First his Cromwell, and George the Third ——." At this point the speaker of the House cried "treason," and the word "treason" was echoed back from many parts of the House. Henry "faltered not for an instant, but rising to a loftier attitude and fixing on the speaker an eye of the most determined fire, finished his sentence with the firmest emphasis on the words, "may profit by their example. If this be treason, make the most of it."

guided, and that is the lamp of experience. I know of no way of judging of the future but by the past. And judging by the past, I wish to know what there has been in the conduct of the British ministry for the last ten years to justify those hopes with which gentlemen have been pleased to solace themselves and the House. Is it that insidious smile with which our petition[1] has been lately received? Trust it not, sir; it will prove a snare to your feet. Suffer not yourselves to be betrayed with a kiss. Ask yourselves how this gracious reception of our petition comports with those warlike preparations which cover our waters and darken our land. Are fleets and armies necessary to a work of love and reconciliation? Have we shown ourselves so unwilling to be reconciled that force must be called in to win back our love? Let us not deceive ourselves, sir. These are the implements of war and subjugation; the last arguments to which kings resort.

I ask gentlemen, sir, what means this martial array, if its purpose be not to force us to submission? Can gentlemen assign any other possible motive for it? Has Great Britain any enemy in this quarter of the world to call for all this accumulation of navies and armies? No, sir, she has none. They are meant for us: they can be meant for no other. They are sent over to bind and rivet upon us those chains which the British ministry have been so long forging. And

[1] The "Petition of Congress to the King," voted on October 25, 1774.

what have we to oppose to them? Shall we try
argument? Sir, we have been trying that for the
last ten years. Have we anything new to offer
upon the subject? Nothing. We have held the
subject up in every light of which it is capable;
but it has been all in vain.

Shall we resort to entreaty and humble supplication? What terms shall we find which have
not been already exhausted? Let us not, I beseech you, sir, deceive ourselves longer. Sir, we
have done everything that could be done, to avert
the storm which is now coming on. We have pe-
titioned; we have remonstrated; we have suppli-
cated; we have prostrated ourselves before the
throne, and have implored its interposition to
arrest the tyrannical hands of the ministry and
Parliament. Our petitions have been slighted;
our remonstrances have produced additional violence and insult; our supplications have been disregarded, and we have been spurned, with con-
tempt, from the foot of the throne!

In vain, after these things, may we indulge the
fond hope of peace and reconciliation. There is
no longer any room for hope. If we wish to be
free—if we mean to preserve inviolate those inestimable privileges for which we have been so
long contending—if we mean not basely to abandon the noble struggle in which we have been so
long engaged, and which we have pledged ourselves never to abandon, until the glorious object
of our contest shall be obtained—we must fight!
I repeat it, sir, we must fight! An appeal to

arms and to the God of Hosts is all that is left us!

They tell us, sir, that we are weak—unable to cope with so formidable an adversary. But when shall we be stronger? Will it be the next week, or the next year? Will it be when we are totally disarmed, and when a British guard shall be stationed in every house? Shall we gather strength by irresolution and inaction? Shall we acquire the means of effectual resistance by lying supinely on our backs and hugging the delusive phantom of hope, until our enemies shall have bound us hand and foot?

Sir, we are not weak if we make a proper use of those means which the God of nature has placed in our power. Three millions of people armed in the holy cause of liberty, and in such a country as that which we possess, are invincible by any force which our enemy can send against us. Besides, sir, we shall not fight our battles alone. There is a just God who presides over the destinies of nations, and who will raise up friends to fight our battles for us. The battle, sir, is not to the strong alone; it is to the vigilant, the active, the brave. Besides, sir, we have no election. If we were base enough to desire it, it is now too late to retire from the contest. There is no retreat but in submission and slavery! Our chains are forged! Their clanking may be heard on the plains of Boston![1] The war is inevitable —and let is come! I repeat it, sir, let it come!

[1] In the autumn of 1774 General Gage had begun to fortify Boston.

It is in vain, sir, to extenuate the matter. Gentlemen may cry, Peace, Peace—but there is no peace. The war is actually begun! The next gale that sweeps from the north will bring to our ears the clash of resounding arms![1] Our brethren are already in the field! Why stand we here idle? What is it that gentlemen wish? What would they have? Is life so dear, or peace so sweet, as to be purchased at the price of chains and slavery? Forbid it, Almighty God! I know not what course others may take; but as for me, give me liberty or give me death![2]

II

SHALL LIBERTY OR EMPIRE BE SOUGHT?[3]

(1788)

THIS, sir, is the language of democracy—that a majority of the community have a right to alter government when found to be oppressive. But how different is the genius of your new Constitution from this! How different from the senti-

[1] The Battle of Lexington occurred less than a month after this speech was delivered—that is, on April 19, 1775.

[2] William Wirt, the biographer of Henry, says that when Henry took his seat, "no murmur of applause was heard. The effect was too deep. After the trance of a moment several members started from their seats. The cry *to arms!* seemed to quiver on every lip, and gleam from every eye. They became impatient of speech. Their souls were on fire for action."

[3] From a speech made on June 5, 1788, in the Virginia Convention, called to ratify the Constitution of the United States.

ments of freemen that a contemptible minority can prevent the good of the majority! If, then, gentlemen standing on this ground are come to that point, that they are willing to bind themselves and their posterity to be oppressed, I am amazed and inexpressibly astonished. If this be the opinion of the majority, I must submit; but to me, sir, it appears perilous and destructive. I can not help thinking so. Perhaps it may be the result of my age. These may be feelings natural to a man of my years, when the American spirit has left him, and his mental powers, like the members of the body, are decayed. If, sir, amendments are left to the twentieth, or tenth part of the people of America, your liberty is gone for ever.

We have heard that there is a great deal of bribery practised in the House of Commons of England, and that many of the members raise themselves to preferments by selling the rights of the whole of the people. But, sir, the tenth part of that body can not continue oppressions on the rest of the people. English liberty is, in this case, on a firmer foundation than American liberty. It will be easily contrived to procure the opposition of one-tenth of the people to any alteration, however judicious. The honorable gentleman who presides told us that, to prevent abuses in our government, we will assemble in convention, recall our delegated powers, and punish our servants for abusing the trust reposed in them. Oh, sir! we should have fine times, indeed, if, to punish tyrants, it were only sufficient to assemble the people! Your arms, wherewith you could defend yourselves, are gone; and you have no longer an aristocratical, no longer a democratical spirit. Did you ever read of any revolution in a nation, brought about by the punishment of those in power, inflicted by those who had no power at all? You read of a riot act in a country which is called one of the freest in the world, where a few neighbors can not assemble without the risk of being shot by a hired soldiery, the engines of despotism. We may see such an act in America.

A standing army we shall have, also, to execute the execrable commands of tyranny; and how are you to punish them? Will you order them to be punished? Who shall obey these orders? Will your mace-bearer be a match for a disciplined regiment? In what situation are we to be? The clause before you gives a power of direct taxation, unbounded and unlimited—an exclusive power of legislation, in all cases whatsoever, for ten miles square, and over all places purchased for the erection of forts, magazines, arsenals, dockyards, etc. What resistance could be made? The attempt would be madness. You will find all the strength of this country in the hands of your enemies; their garrisons will naturally be the strongest places in the country. Your militia is given up to Congress, also, in another part of this plan; they will therefore act as they think proper; all power will be in their own possession. You can not force them to receive their punishment: of what service would militia be to you, when, most probably, you will not have a single musket in the State? For, as arms are to be provided by Congress, they may or may not furnish them.

The honorable gentleman then went on to the figure we make with foreign nations; the contemptible one we make in France and Holland, which, according to the substance of the notes, he attributes to the present feeble government. An opinion has gone forth, we find, that we are contemptible people; the time has been when we were thought otherwise. Under the same despised government we commanded the respect of all Europe; wherefore are we now reckoned otherwise? The American spirit has fled from hence: it has gone to regions where it has never been expected; it has gone to the people of France in search of a splendid government, a strong, energetic government. Shall we imitate the example of those nations who have gone from a simple to a splendid government? Are those nations more worthy of our imitation? What can make an adequate satisfaction to them for the loss they have suffered in attaining such a government— for the loss of their liberty? If we admit this consolidated government, it will be because we like a great, splendid one. Some way or other we must be a great and mighty empire; we must have an army, and a navy, and a number of things. When the American spirit was in its youth, the language of America was different; liberty, sir, was then the primary object.

We are descended from a people whose government was founded on liberty; our glorious forefathers of Great Britain made liberty the foundation of everything. That country is become a great, mighty, and splendid nation; not because their government is strong and energetic, but, sir, because liberty is its direct end and foundation. We drew the spirit of liberty from our British ancestors; by that spirit we have triumphed over every difficulty. But now, sir, the American spirit, assisted by the ropes and chains of consolidation, is about to convert this country into a powerful and mighty empire. If you make the citizens of this country agree to become the subjects of one great consolidated empire of America, your government will not have sufficient energy to keep them together. Such a government is incompatible with the genius of republicanism. There will be no checks, no real balances, in this government. What can avail your specious, imaginary balances, your rope-dancing, chain-rattling, ridiculous ideal checks and contrivances? But, sir, "we are not feared by foreigners; we do not make nations tremble." Would this constitute happiness or secure liberty? I trust, sir, our political hemisphere will ever direct their operations to the security of those objects.

Consider our situation, sir; go to the poor man and ask him what he does. He will inform you that he enjoys the fruits of his labor, under his own fig tree, with his wife and children around him, in peace and security. Go to every other member of society; you will find the same tranquil ease and content; you will find no alarms or disturbances. Why, then, tell us of danger, to terrify us into an adoption of this new form of government? And yet who knows the dangers that this new system may produce? They are out of the sight of the common people; they can not foresee latent consequences. I dread the operation of it on the middling and lower classes of people; it is for them I fear the adoption of this system. I fear I tire the patience of the committee, but I beg to be indulged with a few more observations.

When I thus profess myself an advocate for the liberty of the people, I shall be told I am a designing man, that I am to be a great man, that I am to be a demagog; and many similar illiberal insinuations will be thrown out: but, sir, conscious rectitude outweighs those things with me. I see great jeopardy in this new government. I see none from our present one. I hope some gentleman or other will bring forth, in full array, those dangers, if there be any, that we may see and touch them. I have said that I thought this a consolidated government; I will now prove it. Will the great rights of the people be secured by this government? Suppose it should prove oppressive, how can it be altered? Our Bill of Rights declares that "a majority of the community hath an indubitable,

unalienable, and indefeasible right to reform,
alter, or abolish it, in such manner as shall be
judged most conducive to the public weal.''

The voice of tradition, I trust, will inform
posterity of our struggles for freedom. If our
descendants be worthy the name of Americans
they will preserve and hand down to their latest posterity the transactions of the present
times; and tho I confess my exclamations are
not worthy the hearing, they will see that I
have done my utmost to preserve their liberty,
for I never will give up the power of direct
taxation but for a scourge. I am willing to
give it conditionally—that is, after non-compli-
ance with requisitions. I will do more, sir,
and what I hope will convince the most skep-
tical man that I am a lover of the American
Union: that, in case Virginia shall not make
punctual payment, the control of our custom-
houses and the whole regulation of trade shall
be given to Congress, and that Virginia shall
depend on Congress even for passports, till
Virginia shall have paid the last farthing and
furnished the last soldier.

Nay, sir, there is another alternative to which
I would consent: even that they should strike
us out of the Union and take away from us all
federal privileges till we comply with federal
requisitions; but let it depend upon our own
pleasure to pay our money in the most easy
manner for our people. Were all the States,
more terrible than the mother country, to join

against us, I hope Virginia could defend herself; but, sir, the dissolution of the Union is most abhorrent to my mind. The first thing I have at heart is American liberty; the second thing is American union; and I hope the people of Virginia will endeavor to preserve that union. The increasing population of the Southern States is far greater than that of New England; consequently, in a short time, they will be far more numerous than the people of that country. Consider this and you will find this State more particularly interested to support American liberty and not bind our posterity by an improvident relinquishment of our rights. I would give the best security for a punctual compliance with requisitions; but I beseech gentlemen, at all hazards, not to give up this unlimited power of taxation. The honorable gentleman has told us that these powers given to Congress are accompanied by a judiciary which will correct all. On examination you will find this very judiciary oppressively constructed, your jury trial destroyed, and the judges dependent on Congress.

This Constitution is said to have beautiful features; but when I come to examine these features, sir, they appear to me horribly frightful. Among other deformities, it has an awful squinting; it squints toward monarchy, and does not this raise indignation in the breast of every true American? Your president may easily become king. Your Senate is so imper-

fectly constructed that your dearest rights may
be sacrificed to what may be a small minority;
and a very small minority may continue for
ever unchangeably this government, altho hor-
ridly defective.   Where are your checks in
this government? Your strongholds will be in
the hands of your enemies. It is on a supposition that your American governors shall be
honest that all the good qualities of this government are founded; but its defective and imperfect construction puts it in their power to
perpetrate the worst of mischiefs should they
be bad men; and, sir, would not all the world,
from the Eastern to the Western Hemisphere,
blame our distracted folly in resting our rights
upon the contingency of our rulers being good
or bad? Show me that age and country where
the rights and liberties of the people were
placed on the sole chance of their rulers being
good men without a consequent loss of liberty!
I say that the loss of that dearest privilege has
ever followed, with absolute certainty, every
such mad attempt.

If your American chief be a man of ambition and abilities, how easy is it for him to render himself absolute!   The army is in his
hands, and if he be a man of address, it will be
attached to him, and it will be the subject of
long meditation with him to seize the first
auspicious moment to accomplish his design,
and, sir, will the American spirit solely relieve
you when this happens? I would rather infi-

nitely—and I am sure most of this Convention are of the same opinion—have a king, lords, and commons, than a government so replete with such insupportable evils. If we make a king we may prescribe the rules by which he shall rule his people, and interpose such checks as shall prevent him from infringing them; but the president, in the field, at the head of his army, can prescribe the terms on which he shall reign master, so far that it will puzzle any American ever to get his neck from under the galling yoke. I can not with patience think of this idea. If ever he violate the laws, one of two things will happen: he will come at the head of the army to carry everything before him, or he will give bail, or do what Mr. Chief Justice will order him. If he be guilty, will not the recollection of his crimes teach him to make one bold push for the American throne? Will not the immense difference between being master of everything an being ignominiously tried and punished powerfully excite him to make this bold push? But, sir, where is the existing force to punish him? Can he not, at the head of his army, beat down every opposition? Away with your president! we shall have a king: the army will salute him monarch; your militia will leave you, and assist in making him king, and fight against you: and what have you to oppose this force? What will then become of you and your rights? Will not absolute despotism ensue?

WASHINGTON

I

ON HIS APPOINTMENT AS COMMANDER-IN-CHIEF [1]

(1775)

Born in 1732, died in 1799; Adjutant of Virginia troops in 1751; sent on a mission to the French beyond the Allegheny River in 1753; defended Fort Necessity in 1754; with Braddock at his defeat in 1755; led the advance guard to Fort Duquesne in 1758; Member of he Continental Congresses in 1774–1775; made Commander-in-Chief of the Continental Army in 1775; resigned his commission as Commander-in-Chief in 1783; President of the Constitutional Convention in 1787; elected President of the United States in 1789; re-elected President in 1793; Commander-in-Chief of the Army in 1798.

THO I am truly sensible of the high honor done me in this appointment, yet I feel great distress from a consciousness that my abilities and military experience may not be equal to the

[1] Washington had been chosen general and commander-in-chief by the Continental Congress sitting in Philadelphia on June 15, 1775 —that is, two days before the Battle of Bunker Hill. During the discussion in Congress as to the proper person to receive this appointment, John Adams, in favoring Washington, described him as "a gentleman whose skill and experience as an officer, whose independent fortune, great talents, and excellent universal character, would command the approbation of all America, and unite the cordial exertions of all the Colonies better than any other person in the Union." On the following day the president of Congress officially notified Washington of his appointment, requesting his acceptance. In reply, Washington made the speech here given, as recorded in the journals of Congress.

extensive and important trust. However, as the Congress desire it, I will enter upon the momentous duty, and exert every power I possess in their service and for the support of the glorious cause. I beg they will accept my most cordial thanks for this distinguished testimony of their approbation.

But lest some unlucky event should happen unfavorable to my reputation, I beg it may be remembered by every gentleman in the room that I this day declare, with the utmost sincerity, I do not think myself equal to the command I am honored with.

As to pay, sir, I beg leave to assure the Congress that as no pecuniary consideration could have tempted me to accept this arduous employment at the expense of my domestic ease and happiness, I do not wish to make any profit from it. I will keep an exact account of my expenses. Those, I doubt not, they will discharge, and that is all I desire.[1]

---

[1] Washington kept such an account, and at the end of the war presented it to Congress as drawn up by his own hand. A facsimile of it has been published by Franklin Knight.

II

HIS FIRST INAUGURAL ADDRESS [1]
(1789)

AMONG the vicissitudes incident to life no event could have filled me with greater anxieties than that of which the notification was transmitted by your order, and received on the fourth day of the present month. On the one hand, I was summoned by my country, whose voice I can never hear but with veneration and love, from a retreat which I had chosen with the fondest predilection, and, in my flattering hopes, with an immutable decision, as the asylum of my declining years; a retreat which was rendered every day more necessary as well as more dear to me by the addition of habit to inclination, and of frequent interruptions in my health to the gradual waste committed on it by time; on the other hand, the magnitude and difficulty of the trust to which the voice of my country called me being sufficient to awaken, in the wisest and most experienced of her citizens, a distrustful scrutiny into his qualifications, could not but overwhelm with despondence one who, inheriting inferior endowments from na-

---

[1] Delivered in Federal Hall, Wall Street, New York City, on April 30, 1789. After the oath of office had been administered (on the spot where now stands the statue of Washington in front of the subtreasury building), Washington and the other officials withdrew to the Senate-chamber in Federal Hall, where he delivered this address.

ture, and unpractised in the duties of civil administration, ought to be peculiarly conscious of his own deficiencies.

In this conflict of emotions all I dare aver is that it has been my faithful study to collect my duty from a just appreciation of every circumstance by which it might be affected. All I dare hope is that if, in executing this task, I have been too much swayed by a grateful remembrance of former instances, or by an affectionate sensibility to this transcendent proof of the confidence of my fellow citizens, and have thence too little consulted my incapacity as well as disinclination for the weighty and untried cares before me, my error will be palliated by the motives which misled me, and its consequences be judged by my country with some share of the partiality in which they originated.

Such being the impression under which I have, in obedience to the public summons, repaired to the present station, it would be peculiarly improper to omit, in this first official act, my fervent supplications to that Almighty Being who rules over the universe, who presides in the councils of nations, and whose providential aids can supply every human defect, that His benediction may consecrate to the liberties and happiness of the people of the United States a government instituted by themselves for these essential purposes, and may enable every instrument employed in its administration to execute, with success, the functions allotted to his charge. In tendering this homage to the Great Author of every public and private good, I assure myself that it expresses your sentiments not less than my own nor those of my fellow citizens at large less than either.

No people can be bound to acknowledge and adore the Invisible Hand which conducts the affairs of men more than the people of the United States. Every step by which they have advanced to the character of an independent nation seems to have been distinguished by some token of providential agency. And, in the important revolution just accomplished, in the system of their united government, the tranquil deliberations and voluntary consent of so many distinct communities, from which the event has resulted, can not be compared with the means by which most governments have been established, without some return of pious gratitude, along with a humble anticipation of the future blessings which the past seems to presage. These reflections, arising out of the present crisis, have forced themselves too strongly on my mind to be suppressed. You will join with me, I trust, in thinking that there are none under the influence of which the proceedings of a new and free government can more auspiciously commence.

By the Article establishing the executive department it is made the duty of the president "to recommend to your consideration such measures as he shall judge necessary and expedient." The circumstances under which I now meet you will acquit me from entering into that subject further than to refer you to the great constitutional charter under which we are assembled; and which, in defining your powers, designates the objects to which your attention is to be given. It will be more consistent with those circumstances and far more congenial with the feelings which actuate me, to substitute, in place of a recommendation of particular measures, the tribute that is due to the talents, the rectitude, and the patriotism which adorn the characters selected to devise and adopt them. In these honorable qualifications, I behold the surest pledges, that as, on one side, no local prejudices or attachments, no separate views nor party animosities, will misdirect the comprehensive and equal eye which ought to watch over this great assemblage of communities and interests—so, on another, that the foundations of our national policy will be laid in the pure and immutable principles of private morality; and the preeminence of a free government be exemplified by all the attributes which can win the affections of its citizens and command the respect of the world.

I dwell on this prospect with every satisfaction which an ardent love for my country can inspire; since there is no truth more thoroughly established than that there exists, in the economy and course of nature, an indissoluble union between virtue and happiness—between duty and advantage—between the genuine maxims of an honest and magnanimous policy and the solid rewards of public prosperity and felicity; since we ought to be no less persuaded that the propitious smiles of heaven can never be expected on a nation that disregards the eternal rules of order and right which heaven itself has ordained; and since the preservation of the sacred fire of liberty, and the destiny of the republican model of government, are justly considered as deeply, perhaps as finally staked, on the experiment intrusted to the hands of the American people.

Besides the ordinary objects submitted to your care, it will remain with your judgment to decide how far an exercise of the occasional power delegated by the fifth article of the Constitution is rendered expedient, at the present juncture, by the nature of objections which have been urged against the system, or by the degree of inquietude which has given birth to them. Instead of undertaking particular recommendations on this subject, in which I could be guided by no lights derived from official opportunities, I shall again give way to my entire confidence in your discernment and pursuit of the public good. For I assure myself that, while you carefully avoided every alteration which might endanger the benefits of a united and effective government, or which ought to await the future lessons of experience, a reverence for the characteristic rights of freemen and a regard for the public harmony will sufficiently influence your deliberations on the question how far the former can be more impregnably fortified, or the latter be safely and more advantageously promoted.

To the preceding observations I have one to add, which will be most properly addressed to the House of Representatives. It concerns myself, and will therefore be as brief as possible.

When I was first honored with a call into the service of my country, then on the eve of an arduous struggle for its liberties, the light in which I contemplated my duty required that I should renounce every pecuniary compensation. From this resolution I have in no instance departed. And being still under the impressions which produced it, I must decline, as inapplicable to myself, any share in the personal emoluments which may be indispensably included in a permanent provision for the executive department; and must accordingly pray that the pecuniary estimates for the station in which I am placed may, during my continuation in it, be limited to such actual expenditures as the public good may be thought to require.

Having thus imparted to you my sentiments, as they have been awakened by the occasion which brings us together, I shall take my present leave, but not without resorting once more to the benign Parent of the human race, in humble supplication that, since He has been pleased to favor the American people with opportunities for deliberating in perfect tranquillity, and dispositions for the deciding with unparalleled unanimity, on a form of government for the security of their union and the advancement of their happiness, so His divine blessing may be equally conspicuous in the enlarged views, the temperate consultations, and the wise measures on which the success of this government must depend.

III

HIS FAREWELL ADDRESS[1]
(1796)

THE period for a new election of a citizen to administer the executive government of the United States being not far distant, and the time actually arrived when your thoughts must be employed in designating the person who is to be clothed with that important trust, it appears to me proper, especially as it may conduce to a more distinct expression of the public voice, that I should now apprise you of the resolution I have formed to decline being considered among the number of those out of whom a choice is to be made.

I beg you, at the same time, to do me the

---

[1] September 19, 1796, is the date of the Farewell Address. Here slightly abridged.

justice to be assured that this resolution has not been taken without a strict regard to all the considerations appertaining to the relation which binds a dutiful citizen to his country; and that, in withdrawing the tender of service, which silence in my situation might imply, I am influenced by no diminution of zeal for your future interest, no deficiency of grateful respect for your past kindness, but am supported by a full conviction that the step is compatible with both.

The acceptance of, and continuance hitherto in, the office to which your suffrages have twice called me, have been a uniform sacrifice of inclination to the opinion of duty, and to a deference for what appeared to be your desire. I constantly hoped that it would have been much earlier in my power, consistently with motives which I was not at liberty to disregard, to return to that retirement from which I had been reluctantly drawn. The strength of my inclination to do this, previous to the last election, had even led to the preparation of an address to declare it to you; but mature reflection on the then perplexed and critical posture of our affairs with foreign nations,[1] and the unanimous advice of persons entitled to my confidence, impelled me to abandon the idea.

I rejoice that the state of your concerns, external as well as internal, no longer renders the

[1] Our relations with France during the Revolution and the Reign of Terror are here referred to.

pursuit of inclination incompatible with the sentiment of duty or propriety; and am persuaded, whatever partiality may be retained for my services, that, in the present circumstances of our country, you will not disapprove my determination to retire.

In looking forward to the moment which is intended to terminate the career of my public life, my feelings do not permit me to suspend the deep acknowledgment of that debt of gratitude which I owe to my beloved country for the many honors it has conferred upon me; still more for the steadfast confidence with which it has supported me, and for the opportunities I have thence enjoyed of manifesting my inviolable attachment by services faithful and persevering, tho in usefulness unequal to my zeal. If benefits have resulted to our country from these services let it always be remembered to your praise, and as an instructive example in our annals, that, under circumstances in which the passions, agitated in every direction, were liable to mislead, amid appearances sometimes dubious, vicissitudes of fortune often discouraging, in situations in which not unfrequently want of success has countenanced the spirit of criticism, the constancy of your support was the essential prop of the efforts and a guaranty of the plans by which they were effected. Profoundly penetrated with this idea, I shall carry it with me to my grave as a strong incitement to unceasing vows

that heaven may continue to you the choicest
tokens of its beneficence; that your union and
brotherly affection may be perpetual; that the
free Constitution, which is the work of your
hands, may be sacredly maintained; that its administration in every department may be
stamped with wisdom and virtue; that, in fine,
the happiness of the people of these States, under
the auspices of liberty, may be made complete
by so careful a preservation and so prudent a
use of this blessing as will acquire to them the
glory of recommending it to the applause, the
affection, and adoption of every nation which
is yet a stranger to it.

Here, perhaps, I ought to stop. But a
solicitude for your welfare which can not end
but with my life, and the apprehension of danger natural to that solicitude, urge me, on an
occasion like the present, to offer to your solemn contemplation and to recommend to your
frequent review some sentiments which are the
result of much reflection of no inconsiderable
observation, and which appear to me all-
important to the permanency of your felicity as
a people. These will be offered to you with
the more freedom as you can only see in them
the disinterested warnings of a parting friend
who can possibly have no personal motive to
bias his counsel. Nor can I forget, as an encouragement to it, your indulgent reception of
my sentiments on a former and not dissimilar
occasion.

Interwoven as is the love of liberty with every ligament of your hearts, no recommendation of mine is necessary to fortify or confirm the attachment.

The unity of government which constitutes you one people is also now dear to you. It is justly so, for it is a main pillar in the edifice of your real independence; the support of your tranquillity at home, your peace abroad; of your safety; of your prosperity; of that very liberty which you so highly prize. But as it is easy to foresee that from different causes and from different quarters much pains will be taken, many artifices employed, to weaken in your minds the conviction of this truth; as this is the point in your political fortress against which the batteries of internal and external enemies will be most constantly and actively (tho often covertly and insidiously) directed, it is of infinite moment that you should properly estimate the immense value of your national Union to your collective and individual happiness; that you should cherish a cordial, habitual, and immovable attachment to it; accustoming yourselves to think and speak of it as the palladium of your political safety and prosperity; watching for its preservation with jealous anxiety; discountenancing whatever may suggest even a suspicion that it can in any event be abandoned; and indignantly frowning upon the first dawning of every attempt to alienate any portion of our country from the rest, or to enfeeble the sacred ties which now link together the various parts.

For this you have every inducement of sympathy and of interest. Citizens, either by birth or choice, of a common country, that country has a right to concentrate your affections. The name of AMERICAN which belongs to you in your national capacity must always exalt the just pride of patriotism more than any appellation derived from local discriminations. With slight shades of difference you have the same religion, manners, habits, and political principles. You have in a common cause fought and triumphed together; the independence and liberty you possess are the work of joint counsels and joint efforts, of common dangers, sufferings, and successes.

But these considerations, however powerfully they address themselves to your sensibility, are greatly outweighed by those which apply more immediately to your interest. Here every portion of our country finds the most commanding motives for carefully guarding and preserving the union of the whole.

The North, in an unrestrained intercourse with the South, protected by the equal laws of a common government, finds in the productions of the latter great additional resources of maritime and commercial enterprise and precious materials of manufacturing industry. The South, in the same intercourse, benefiting by the agency of the North, sees its agriculture grow and its commerce expand. Turning partly into its own channels the seamen of the North, it finds its particular navigation invigorated, and while it contributes, in different ways, to nourish and increase the general mass of the national navigation, it looks forward to the protection of a maritime strength, to which itself is unequally adapted. The East, in a like intercourse with the West, already finds—and in a progressive improvement of interior communications by land and water will more and more find—a valuable vent for the commodities which it brings from abroad or manufactures at home. The West derives from the East supplies requisite to its growth and comfort, and what is perhaps of still greater consequence, it must of necessity owe the secure enjoyment of indispensable outlets for its own productions to the weight, influence, and the future maritime strength of the Atlantic side of the Union, directed by an indissoluble community of interest as one nation. Any other tenure by which the West can hold this essential advantage, whether derived from its own separate strength or from an apostate and unnatural connection with any foreign power, must be intrinsically precarious.

While, then, every part of our country thus feels an immediate and particular interest in union, all the parts combined can not fail to find in the united mass of means and efforts greater strength, greater resource, proportionably greater security from external danger, a less frequent interruption of their peace by foreign nations; and, what is of inestimable value, they must derive from union an exemption from those broils and wars between themselves which so frequently afflict neighboring countries not tied together by the same governments, which their own rivalships alone would be sufficient to produce, but which opposite foreign alliances, attachments, and intrigues would stimulate and embitter. Hence, likewise, they will avoid the necessity of those overgrown military establishments, which, under any form of government, are inauspicious to liberty, and which are to be regarded as particularly hostile to republican liberty. In this sense it is that your union ought to be considered as a main prop of your liberty, and that the love of the one ought to endear to you the preservation of the other.

These considerations speak a persuasive language to every reflecting and virtuous mind, and exhibit the continuance of the Union as a primary object of patriotic desire. Is there a doubt whether a common government can embrace so large a sphere? Let experience solve it. To listen to mere speculation in such a case were criminal. We are authorized to hope that a proper organization of the whole, with the auxiliary agency of governments for the respective subdivisions, will afford a happy issue to the experiment. It is well worth a fair and full experiment. With such powerful and obvious motives to union affecting all parts of our country, while experience shall not have demonstrated its impracticability, there will always be reason to distrust the patriotism of those who in any quarter may endeavor to weaken its bands.

In contemplating the causes which may disturb our Union it occurs as a matter of serious concern that any ground should have been furnished for characterizing parties by geographical discriminations, Northern and Southern, Atlantic and Western; whence designing men may endeavor to excite a belief that there is a real difference of local interests and views. One of the expedients of party to acquire influence within particular districts is to misrepresent the opinions and aims of other districts. You can not shield yourselves too much against the jealousies and heartburnings which spring from these misrepresentations; they tend to render alien to each other those who ought to be bound together by fraternal affection. The inhabitants of our Western country have lately had a useful lesson on this head; they have seen, in the negotiation by the executive, and in the unanimous ratification by the Senate, of the treaty with Spain,[1] and in the universal satisfaction at that event throughout the United States, a decisive proof how unfounded were

[1] This treaty related to the navigation of the Mississippi by people of both nations.

the suspicions propagated among them of a policy in the general government and in the Atlantic States unfriendly to their interests in regard to the Mississippi; they have been witnesses to the formation of two treaties, that with Great Britain[1] and that with Spain, which secure to them everything they could desire, in respect to our foreign relations, toward confirming their prosperity. Will it not be their wisdom to rely for the preservation of these advantages on the Union by which they were procured? Will they not henceforth be deaf to those advisers, if such there are, who would sever them from their brethren, and connect them with aliens?

To the efficacy and permanency of your Union a government for the whole is indispensable. No alliances, however strict, between the parts can be an adequate substitute; they must inevitably experience the infractions and interruptions which all alliances in all times have experienced. Sensible of this momentous truth, you have improved upon your first essay by the adoption of a constitution of government better caluculated than your former for an intimate union and for the efficacious management of your common concerns. This government, the offspring of your own choice, uninfluenced and unawed, adopted upon full investigation and mature deliberation, completely free in its

---

[1] The Jay Treaty of August 18, 1795.

principles, in the distribution of its powers,
uniting security with energy, and containing
within itself a provision for its own amendment, has a just claim to your confidence and
your support. Respect for its authority, compliance with its laws, acquiescence in its measures, are duties enjoined by the fundamental
maxims of true liberty. The basis of our political systems is the right of the people to
make and to alter their constitutions of government. But the constitution which at any
time exists till changed by an explicit and
authentic act of the whole people is sacredly
obligatory upon all. The very idea of the
power and the right of the people to establish
government presupposes the duty of every individual to obey the established government.

All obstructions to the execution of the laws,
all combinations and associations, under whatever plausible character, with the real design
to direct, control, counteract, or awe the regular deliberation and action of the constituted
authorities, are destructive of this fundamental
principle, and of fatal tendency. They serve
to organize faction, to give it an artificial and
extraordinary force; to put, in the place of
the delegated will of the nation, the will of a
party, often a small but artful and enterpri-
sing minority of the community; and, according
to the alternate triumphs of different parties,
to make the public administration the mirror of
the ill-concerted and incongruous projects of

fashion, rather than the organs of consistent and wholesome plans digested by common councils, and modified by mutual interests.

However combinations or associations of the above description may now and then answer popular ends, they are likely, in the course of time and things, to become potent engines, by which cunning, ambitious, and unprincipled men will be enabled to subvert the power of the people, and to usurp for themselves the reins of government, destroying afterward the very engines which have lifted them to unjust dominion.

Toward the preservation of your government and the permanency of your present happy state it is requisite not only that you steadily discountenance irregular oppositions to its acknowledged authority, but also that you resist with care the spirit of innovation upon its principles, however specious the pretexts. One method of assault may be to affect, in the forms of the Constitution, alterations which will impair the energy of the system, and thus to undermine what can not be directly overthrown. In all the changes to which you may be invited, remember that time and habit are at least as necessary to fix the true character of governments as of other human institutions; that experience is the surest standard by which to test the real tendency of the existing constitution of a country; that facility in changes, upon the credit of mere hypothesis and opinion, exposes to perpetual change, from the endless variety of hypothesis and opinion; and remember especially that for the efficient management of your common interests, in a country so extensive as ours, a government of as much vigor as is consistent with the perfect security of liberty is indispensable. Liberty itself will find in such a government, with powers properly distributed and adjusted, its surest guardian. It is, indeed, little else than a name where the government is too feeble to withstand the enterprises of faction, to confine each member of the society within the limits prescribed by the laws, and to maintain all in the secure and tranquil enjoyment of the rights of person and property.

I have already intimated to you the danger of parties in the State, with particular reference to the founding of them on geographical discrimination. Let me now take a more comprehensive view, and warn you in the most solemn manner against the baneful effects of the spirit of party generally.

This spirit, unfortunately, is inseparable from our nature, having its root in the strongest passions of the human mind. It exists under different shapes in all governments, more or less stifled, controlled, or repressed; but in those of the popular form it is seen in its greatest rankness, and is truly their worst enemy.

The alternate domination of one faction over another, sharpened by the spirit of revenge, natural to party dissension, which in different ages and countries has perpetrated the most horrid enormities, is itself a frightful despotism. But this leads at length to a more formal and permanent despotism. The disorders and miseries which result gradually incline the minds of men to seek security and repose in the absolute power of an individual, and sooner or later the chief of some prevailing faction, more able or more fortunate than his competitors, turns this disposition to the purposes of his own elevation, on the ruins of public liberty.

Without looking forward to an extremity of this kind (which nevertheless ought not to be entirely out of sight), the common and continued mischiefs of the spirit of party are sufficient to make it the interest and duty of a wise people to discourage and restrain it.

It serves always to distract the public councils and enfeeble the public administration. It agitates the community with ill-founded jealousies and false alarms; kindles the animosity of one part against another; foments, occasionally, riot and insurrection. It opens the doors to foreign influence and corruption, which find a facilitated access to the government itself through the channels of party passions. Thus the policy and the will of one country are subjected to the policy and will of another.

There is an opinion that parties in free countries are useful checks upon the administration of the government and serve to keep alive the spirit of liberty. This within certain limits is probably true, and in governments of a monarchical cast, patriotism may look with indulgence, if not with favor, upon the spirit of party. But in those of the popular character, in governments purely elective, it is a spirit not to be encouraged. From their natural tendency it is certain there will always be enough of that spirit for every salutary purpose. And there being constant danger of excess, the effort ought to be by force of public opinion to mitigate and assuage it. A fire not to be quenched, it demands a uniform vigilance to prevent its bursting into a flame, lest, instead of warming, it should consume.

It is important, likewise, that the habits of thinking in a free country should inspire caution, in those intrusted with its administration, to confine themselves within their respective constitutional spheres, avoiding in the exercise of the powers of one department to encroach upon another. The spirit of encroachment tends to consolidate the powers of all the departments in one, and thus to create, whatever the form of government, a real despotism. A just estimate of that love of power and proneness to abuse it which predominates in the human heart is sufficient to satisfy us of the truth of this position. The necessity of reciprocal checks in the exercise of political power by dividing and distributing it into different depositories, and constituting each the guardian of the public weal against invasions by the others, has been evinced by experiments, ancient and modern, some of them in our country and under our own eyes. To preserve them must be as necessary as to institute them. If, in the opinion of the people, the distribution or modification of the constitutional powers be in any particular wrong, let it be corrected by an amendment in the way which the Constitution designates. But let there be no change by usurpation; for tho this, in one instance, may be the instrument of good, it is the customary weapon by which free governments are destroyed. The precedent must always greatly overbalance in permanent evil any partial or transient benefit which the use can at any time yield.

Of all the dispositions and habits which lead to political prosperity, religion and morality are indispensable supports. In vain would that man claim the tribute of patriotism who should labor to subvert these great pillars of human happiness, these firmest props of the duties of men and citizens. The mere politician, equally with the pious man, ought to respect and to cherish them. A volume could not trace all their connections with private and public felicity. Let it simply be asked, Where is the security for property, for reputation, for life, if the sense of religious obligation desert the oaths, which are the instruments of investigation in courts of justice? And let us with caution indulge the supposition that morality can be maintained without religion. Whatever may be conceded to the influence of refined education on minds of peculiar structure, reason and experience both forbid us to expect that national morality can prevail in exclusion of religious principle.

It is substantially true that virtue or morality is a necessary spring of popular government. The rule, indeed, extends with more or less force to every species of free government. Who that is a sincere friend to it can look with indifference upon attempts to shake the foundation of the fabric?

Promote, then, as an object of primary importance, institutions for the general diffusion of knowledge. In proportion as the structure of a government gives force to public opinion it is essential that public opinion should be enlightened.

As a very important source of strength and security, cherish public credit. One method of preserving it is to use it as sparingly as possible; avoiding occasions of expense by cultivating peace, but remembering also that timely disbursements to prepare for danger frequently prevent much greater disbursements to repel it; avoiding likewise the accumulation of debt, not only by shunning occasions of expense, but by vigorous exertion in time of peace to discharge the debts, which unavoidable wars may have occasioned, not ungenerously throwing upon posterity the burden which we ourselves ought to bear. The execution of these maxims belongs to your representatives, but it is necessary that public opinion should cooperate. To facilitate to them the performance of their duty it is essential that you should practically bear in mind that toward the payment of debts there must be revenue; that to have revenue there must be taxes; that no taxes can be devised which are not more or less inconvenient and unpleasant; that the intrinsic embarrassment, inseparable from the selection of the proper objects (which is always a choice of difficulties), ought to be a decisive motive for a candid construction of the conduct of the government in making it, and for a spirit of acquiescence in the measures for obtaining revenue which the public exigencies may at any time dictate.

Observe good faith and justice toward all nations; cultivate peace and harmony with all. Religion and morality enjoin this conduct, and can it be that good policy does not equally enjoin it? It will be worthy of a free, enlightened, and, at no distant period, a great nation, to give to mankind the magnanimous and novel example of a people always guided by an exalted justice and benevolence. Who can doubt that, in the course of time and things, the fruits of such a plan would richly repay any temporary advantages which might be lost by a steady adherence to it? Can it be that providence has not connected the permanent felicity of a nation with its virtue? The experiment, at least, is recommended by every sentiment which ennobles human nature. Alas! is it rendered impossible by its vices?

In the execution of such a plan nothing is more essential than that permanent, inveterate antipathies against particular nations and passionate attachments for others should be excluded, and that, in place of them, just and amicable feelings toward all should be cultivated. The nation which indulges toward another an habitual hatred or an habitual fondness is in some degree a slave. It is a slave to its animosity or to its affection, either of which is sufficient to lead it astray from its duty and its interest. Antipathy in one nation against another disposes each more readily to offer insult and injury, to lay hold of slight causes of umbrage, and to be haughty and intractable, when accidental or trifling occasions of dispute occur. Hence, frequent collisions; obstinate, envenomed, and bloody contests. The nation, prompted by ill will and resentment, sometimes impels to war the government, contrary to the best calculations of policy. The government sometimes participates in the national propensity, and adopts through passion what reason would reject; at other times it makes the animosity of the nation subservient to projects of hostility instigated by pride, ambition, and other sinister and pernicious motives. The peace often, sometimes perhaps the liberty, of nations has been the victim.

So, likewise, a passionate attachment of one nation for another produces a variety of evils. Sympathy for the favorite nation, facilitating the illusion of an imaginary common interest in cases where no real common interest exists, and infusing into one the enmities of the other, betrays the former into a participation in the quarrels and wars of the latter, without adequate inducement or justification. It leads also to concessions to the favorite nation of privileges denied to others, which is apt doubly to injure the nation making the concessions by unnecessarily parting with what ought to have been retained, and by exciting jealousy, ill will, and a disposition to retaliate, in the parties from whom equal privileges are withheld. And it gives to ambitious, corrupted, or deluded citizens (who devote themselves to the favorite nation), facility to betray or sacrifice the interests of their own country without odium, sometimes even with popularity; gilding with the appearances of a virtuous sense of obligation, a commendable deference for public opinion, or a laudable zeal for public good, the base or foolish compliances of ambition, corruption, or infatuation.

As avenues to foreign influence in innumerable ways, such attachments are particularly alarming to the truly enlightened and independent patriot. How many opportunities do they

afford to tamper with domestic factions, to practise the arts of seduction, to mislead public
opinion, to influence or awe the public councils! Such an attachment of a small or weak
toward a great and powerful nation dooms the
former to be the satellite of the latter.

Against the insidious wiles of foreign influence (I conjure you to believe me, fellow citizens), the jealousy of a free people ought to be
constantly awake, since history and experience
prove that foreign influence is one of the most
baneful foes of republican government. But
that jealousy, to be useful, must be impartial,
else it becomes the instrument of the very influence to be avoided, instead of a defense against
it. Excessive partiality for one foreign nation
and excessive dislike of another cause those
whom they actuate to see danger only on one
side, and serve to veil and even second the arts
of influence on the other. Real patriots, who
may resist the intrigues of the favorite, are liable to become suspected and odious; while its
tools and dupes usurp the applause and confidence of the people, to surrender their interests.

The great rule of conduct for us, in regard to
foreign nations, is, in extending our commercial
relations, to have with them as little political
connection as possible. So far as we have already formed engagements, let them be fulfilled
with perfect good faith. Here let us stop.

Europe has a set of primary interests which
to us have none, or a very remote, relation.

Hence she must be engaged in frequent controversies, the causes of which are essentially foreign to our concerns. Hence, therefore, it must be unwise in us to implicate ourselves, by artificial ties, in the ordinary vicissitudes of her politics or the ordinary combinations and collisions of her friendships or enmities.

Our detached and distant situation invites and enables us to pursue a different course. If we remain one people, under an efficient government the period is not far off when we may defy material injury from external annoyance; when we may take such an attitude as will cause the neutrality we may at any time resolve upon to be scrupulously respected; when belligerent nations, under the impossibility of making acquisitions upon us, will not lightly hazard the giving us provocation; when we may choose peace or war, as our interest, guided by justice, shall counsel.

Why forego the advantages of so peculiar a situation? Why quit our own to stand upon foreign ground? Why, by interweaving our destiny with that of any part of Europe, entangle our peace and prosperity in the toils of European ambition, rivalship, interest, humor, or caprice?

It is our true policy to steer clear of permanent alliances with any portion of the foreign world—so far, I mean, as we are now at liberty to do it; for let me not be understood as capable of patronizing infidelity to existing engagements. I hold the maxim no less applicable to public than to private affairs, that honesty is always the best policy. I repeat it, therefore, let those engagements be observed in their genuine sense. But, in my opinion, it is unnecessary and would be unwise to extend them.

Taking care always to keep ourselves, by suitable establishments, on a respectable defensive posture, we may safely trust to temporary alliances for extraordinary emergencies.

Harmony, liberal intercourse with all nations, are recommended by policy, humanity, and interest. But even our commercial policy should hold an equal and impartial hand; neither seeking nor granting exclusive favors or preferences; consulting the natural course of things; diffusing and diversifying by gentle means the streams of commerce, but forcing nothing; establishing, with powers so disposed, in order to give trade a stable course, to define the rights of our merchants, and to enable the government to support them, conventional rules of intercourse, the best that present circumstances and mutual opinion will permit, but temporary, and liable to be from time to time abandoned or varied, as experience and circumstances shall dictate; constantly keeping in view that it is folly in one nation to look for disinterested favors from another; that it must pay with a portion of its independence for whatever it may accept under that character; that, by such acceptance, it may place itself in the condition of having given equivalents for nominal favors, and yet of being reproached with ingratitude for not giving more. There can be no greater error than to expect or calculate upon real favors from nation to nation. It is an illusion which experience must cure, which a just pride ought to discard.

In offering to you, my countrymen, these counsels of an old and affectionate friend, I dare not hope they will make the strong and lasting impression I could wish; that they will control the usual current of the passions, or prevent our nation from running the course which has hitherto marked the destiny of nations. But if I may even flatter myself that they may be productive of some partial benefit, some occasional good; that they may now and then recur to moderate the fury of party spirit, to warn against the mischiefs of foreign intrigue, to guard against the impostures of pretended patriotism: this hope will be a full recompense for the solicitude for your welfare by which they have been dictated.

Tho in reviewing the incidents of my administration I am unconscious of intentional error, I am nevertheless too sensible of my defects not to think it probable that I may have committed many errors. Whatever they may be, I fervently beseech the Almighty to avert or mitigate the evils to which they may tend. I shall also carry with me the hope that my country will never cease to view them with indulgence;

and that, after forty-five years of my life dedicated to its service with an upright zeal, the faults of incompetent abilities will be consigned to oblivion, as myself must soon be to the mansions of rest.

Relying on its kindness in this as in other things, and actuated by that fervent love toward it which is so natural to a man who views in it the native soil of himself and his progenitors for several generations, I anticipate with pleasing expectation that retreat in which I promise myself to realize, without alloy, the sweet enjoyment of partaking in the midst of my fellow citizens the benign influence of good laws under a free government, the ever favorite object of my heart, and the happy reward, as I trust, of our mutual cares, labors, and dangers.

SAMUEL ADAMS

ON AMERICAN INDEPENDENCE[1]
(1776)

Born in 1722, died in 1803; Delegate to the First Continental Congress in 1774; Signer of the Declaration of Independence in 1776; Member of the Massachusetts Convention ratifying the Constitution in 1788, Governor of Massachusetts in 1794.

OUR forefathers, 'tis said, consented to be subject to the laws of Great Britain. I will not at the present time dispute it, nor mark out the limits and conditions of their submission; but will it be denied that they contracted to pay obedience and to be under the control of Great Britain because it appeared to them most beneficial in their then present circumstances and situations? We, my countrymen, have the same right to consult and provide for our happiness which they had to promote theirs. If they had a view to posterity in their contracts, it must have been to advance the felicity of their descendants. If they erred in their expectations and prospects, we can never be condemned for a conduct which they would have recommended had they foreseen our present condition.

Ye darkeners of counsel, who would make

[1] From a speech delivered at the State House in Philadelphia, "to a very numerous audience," on August 1, 1776. Abridged.

the property, lives, and religion of millions depend on the evasive interpretations of musty
parchments; who would send us to antiquated
charters of uncertain and contradictory meaning, to prove that the present generation are
not bound to be victims to cruel and unforgiv-
ing despotism,—tell us whether our pious and
generous ancestors bequeathed to us the miserable privilege of having the rewards of our
honesty, industry, the fruits of those fields
which they purchased and bled for, wrested
from us at the will of men over whom we have
no check. Did they contract for us that, with
folded arms, we should expect that justice and
mercy from brutal and inflamed invaders which
have been denied to our supplications at the
foot of the throne? Were we to hear our
character as a people ridiculed with indifference? Did they promise for us that our meek-
ness and patience should be insulted, our coasts
harassed, our towns demolished and plundered,
and our wives and offspring exposed to naked-
ness, hunger, and death, without our feeling
the resentment of men, and exerting those
powers of self-preservation which God has
given us?

No man had once a greater veneration for
Englishmen than I entertained. They were
dear to me as branches of the same parental
trunk, and partakers of the same religion and
laws; I still view with respect the remains of
the Constitution as I would a lifeless body

which had once been animated by a great and heroic soul. But when I am aroused by the din of arms; when I behold legions of foreign assassins paid by Englishmen to imbrue their hands in our blood; when I tread over the un-coffined bodies of my countrymen, neighbors, and friends; when I see the locks of a vener-able father torn by savage hands, and a feeble mother, clasping her infants to her bosom, and on her knees imploring their lives from her own slaves, whom Englishmen have allured to treachery and murder; when I behold my coun-try, once the seat of industry, peace, and plenty, changed by Englishmen to a theater of blood and misery, Heaven forgive me if I can not root out those passions which it has im-planted in my bosom, and detest submission to a people who have either ceased to be hu-man, or have not virtue enough to feel their own wretchedness and servitude!

Men who content themselves with the sem-blance of truth, and a display of words talk much of our obligations to Great Britain for protection. Had she a single eye to our advan-tage? A nation of shopkeepers[1] are very sel-dom so interested. Let us not be so amused with words! the extension of her commerce was her object. When she defended our coasts, she fought for her customers, and convoyed our

---

[1] Napoleon afterward used this phrase and has often been credited with its authorship.

ships loaded with wealth, which we had acquired for her by our industry. She has treated us as beasts of burden, whom the lordly masters cherish that they may carry a greater load. Let us inquire also against whom she has protected us? Against her own enemies with whom we had no quarrel, or only on her account, and against whom we always readily exerted our wealth and strength when they were required. Were these Colonies backward in giving assistance to Great Britain, when they were called upon in 1739 to aid the expedition against Cartagena? They at that time sent three thousand men to join the British army, altho the war commenced without their consent.

But the last war, 'tis said, was purely American. This is a vulgar error, which, like many others, has gained credit by being confidently repeated. The dispute between the courts of Great Britain and France related to the limits of Canada and Nova Scotia. The controverted territory was not claimed by any in the Colonies, but by the crown of Great Britain. It was therefore their own quarrel. The infringement of a right which England had, by the treaty of Utrecht, of trading in the Indian country of Ohio, was another cause of the war. The French seized large quantities of British manufactures and took possession of a fort which a company of British merchants and factors had erected for the security of their commerce. The war was therefore waged in defense of lands claimed by the Crown, and for the protection of British property. The French at that time had no quarrel with America, and, as appears by letters sent from their commander-in-chief to some of the Colonies, wished to remain in peace with us.

The part, therefore, which we then took, and the miseries to which we exposed ourselves ought to be charged to our affection to Britain. These Colonies granted more than their proportion to the support of the war. They raised, clothed, and maintained nearly twenty-five thousand men, and so sensible were the people of England of our great exertions that a message was annually sent to the House of Commons purporting "that his majesty, being highly satisfied with the zeal and vigor with which his faithful subjects in North America had exerted themselves in defense of his majesty's just rights and possessions, recommends it to the House to take the same into consideration and enable him to give them a proper compensation."

But what purpose can arguments of this kind answer? Did the protection we received annul our rights as men, and lay us under an obligation of being miserable?

Who among you, my countrymen, that is a father, would claim authority to make your child a slave because you had nourished him in infancy?

'Tis a strange species of generosity which requires a return infinitely more valuable than anything it could have bestowed; that demands as a reward for a defense of our property a surrender of those inestimable privileges to the arbitrary will of vindictive tyrants, which alone give value to that very property.

Courage, then, my countrymen; our contest is not only whether we ourselves shall be free, but whether there shall be left to mankind an asylum on earth for civil and religious liberty. Dismissing, therefore, the justice of our cause as incontestable, the only question is, What is best for us to pursue in our present circumstances?

The doctrine of dependence on Great Britain is, I believe, generally exploded; but as I would attend to the honest weakness of the simplest of men, you will pardon me if I offer a few words on that subject.

We are now on this continent, to the astonishment of the world, three millions of souls united in one cause. We have large armies, well disciplined and appointed, with commanders inferior to none in military skill, and superior in activity and zeal. We are furnished with arsenals and stores beyond our most sanguine expectations, and foreign nations are waiting to crown our success by their alliances. There are instances of, I would say, an almost astonishing providence in our favor; our success has staggered our enemies, and almost given faith to infidels; so we may truly say it is not our own arm which has saved us.

The hand of Heaven appears to have led us on to be, perhaps, humble instruments and means in the great providential dispensation which is completing. We have fled from the political Sodom; let us not look back lest we perish and become a monument of infamy and derision to the world. For can we ever expect more unanimity and a better preparation for defense; more infatuation of counsel among our enemies, and more valor and zeal among ourselves? The same force and resistance which are sufficient to procure us our liberties will secure us a glorious independence and support us in the dignity of free imperial States. We can not suppose that our opposition has made a corrupt and dissipated nation more friendly to America, or created in them a greater respect for the rights of mankind. We can therefore expect a restoration and establishment of our privileges, and a compensation for the injuries we have received from their want of power, from their fears, and not from their virtues. The unanimity and valor which will effect an honorable peace can render a future contest for our liberties unnecessary. He who has strength to chain down the wolf is a madman if he let him loose without drawing his teeth and paring his nails.

From the day on which an accommodation takes place between England and America, on any other terms than as independent States, I shall date the ruin of this country. A politic minister will study to lull us into security by granting us the full extent of our petitions. The warm sunshine of influence would melt down the virtue which the violence of the storm rendered more firm and unyielding. In a state of tranquillity, wealth, and luxury, our descendants would forget the arts of war and the noble activity and zeal which made their ancestors invincible. Every art of corruption would be employed to loosen the bond of union which renders our resistance formidable. When the spirit of liberty, which now animates our hearts and gives success to our arms, is extinct, our numbers will accelerate our ruin and render us easier victims to tyranny. Ye abandoned minions of an infatuated ministry, if peradventure any should yet remain among us, remember that a Warren and Montgomery are numbered among the dead. Contemplate the mangled bodies of your countrymen, and then say, What should be the reward of such sacrifices? Bid us and our posterity bow the knee, supplicate the friendship, and plow, and sow, and reap, to glut the avarice of the men who have let loose on us the dogs of war to riot in our blood and hunt us from the face of the earth? If ye love wealth better than liberty, the tranquillity of servitude than the animating contest of freedom—go from us in peace. We ask not your counsels or arms. Crouch down and lick the hands which feed you. May your chains sit lightly upon you, and may posterity forget that ye were our countrymen!

To unite the supremacy of Great Britain and the liberty of America is utterly impossible. So vast a continent and of such a distance from the seat of empire will every day grow more unmanageable. The motion of so unwieldy a body can not be directed with any despatch and uniformity without committing to the Parliament of Great Britain powers inconsistent with our freedom. The authority and force which would be absolutely necessary for the preservation of the peace and good order of this continent would put all our valuable rights within the reach of that nation.

As the administration of government requires firmer and more numerous supports in proportion to its extent, the burdens imposed on us would be excessive, and we should have the melancholy prospect of their increasing on our posterity. The scale of officers, from the rapacious and needy commissioner to the haughty governor, and from the governor, with his hungry train, to perhaps a licentious and prodigal viceroy, must be upheld by you and your children. The fleets and armies which will be employed to silence your murmurs and complaints must be supported by the fruits of your industry.

Britain is now, I will suppose, the seat of liberty and virtue, and its legislature consists of a body of able and independent men who govern with wisdom and justice. The time may come when all will be reversed; when its excellent constitution of government will be subverted; when, pressed by debts and taxes, it will be greedy to draw to itself an increase of revenue from every distant province in order to ease its own burdens; when the influence of the crown, strengthened by luxury and a universal profligacy of manners, will have tainted every heart, broken down every fence of liberty and rendered us a nation of tame and contented vassals; when a general election will be nothing but a general auction of boroughs, and when the Parliament, the grand council of the nation, and once the faithful guardian of the State, and a terror to evil ministers, will be degenerated into a body if sycophants, dependent and venal, always ready to confirm any measures, and little more than a public court for registering royal edicts.

Such, it is possible, may some time or other be the state of Great Britain. What will, at that period, be the duty of the Colonies? Will they be still bound to unconditional submission? Must they always continue an appendage to our government and follow it implicitly through every change that can happen to it? Wretched condition, indeed, of millions of freemen as good as ourselves! Will you say that we now govern equitably, and that there is no danger of such revolution? Would to God that this

were true! But you will not always say the
same. Who shall judge whether we govern
equitably or not? Can you give the Colonies
any security that such a period will never
come? No. *The period, countrymen, is already
come!* The calamities were at our door. The
rod of oppression was raised over us. We were
roused from our slumbers, and may we never
sink into repose until we can convey a clear
and undisputed inheritance to our posterity!
This day we are called upon to give a glorious
example of what the wisest and best of men
were rejoiced to view only in speculation. This
day presents the world with the most august
spectacle that its annals ever unfolded—millions of freemen, deliberately and voluntarily
forming themselves into a society for their
common defense and common happiness. Immortal spirits of Hampden, Locke, and Sidney,
will it not add to your benevolent joys to behold your posterity rising to the dignity of men,
and evincing to the world the reality and expediency of your systems, and in the actual enjoyment of that equal liberty, which you were
happy when on earth in delineating and recommending to mankind?

Other nations have received their laws from
conquerors; some are indebted for a constitution to the suffering of their ancestors through
revolving centuries. The people of this country, alone, have formally and deliberately
chosen a government for themselves, and with

open and uninfluenced consent bound themselves into a social compact. Here no man proclaims his birth or wealth as a title to honorable distinction, or to sanctify ignorance and vice with the name of hereditary authority. He who has most zeal and ability to promote public felicity, let him be the servant of the public. This is the only line of distinction drawn by nature. Leave the bird of night to the obscurity for which nature intended him, and expect only from the eagle to brush the clouds with his wings and look boldly in the face of the sun.

If there is any man so base or so weak as to prefer a dependence on Great Britain to the dignity and happiness of living a member of a free and independent nation, let me tell him that necessity now demands what the generous principle of patriotism should have dictated.

We have no other alternative than independence, or the most ignominious and galling servitude. The legions of our enemies thicken on our plains; desolation and death mark their bloody career, while the mangled corpses of our countrymen seem to cry out to us as a voice from heaven.

Our Union is now complete; our Constitution composed, established, and approved. You are now the guardians of your own liberties. We may justly address you as the decemviri did the Romans, and say: "Nothing that we propose can pass into a law without your consent. Be yourselves, O Americans, the authors of those laws on which your happiness depends.''

You have now in the field armies sufficient to repel the whole force of your enemies and their base and mercenary auxiliaries. The hearts of your soldiers beat high with the spirit of freedom; they are animated with the justice of their cause, and while they grasp their swords can look up to Heaven for assistance. Your adversaries are composed of wretches who laugh at the rights of humanity, who turn religion into derision, and would, for higher wages, direct their swords against their leaders or their country. Go on, then, in your generous enterprise with gratitude to Heaven for past success, and confidence of it in the future. For my own part I ask no greater blessing than to share with you the common danger and common glory. If I have a wish dearer to my soul than that my ashes may be mingled with those of a Warren and Montgomery, it is that these American States may never cease to be free and independent.

WILLIAM PINKNEY

FOR THE RELIEF OF SLAVES [1]

(1788)

Born in 1764, died in 1822; Minister to Great Britain in 1806; Attorney-General in 1811; Member of Congress in 1815; Minister to Naples in 1816; Minister to Russia in 1816; United States Senator in 1820.

BEFORE I proceed to deliver my sentiments on the subject-matter of the report under consideration, I must entreat the members of this House to hear me with patience, and not to condemn what I may happen to advance in support of the opinion I have formed, until they shall have heard me out. I am conscious, sir, that upon this occasion I have long-established principles to combat and deep-rooted prejudices to defeat; that I have fears and apprehensions to silence, which the acts of former legislatures have sanctioned, and that (what is equivalent to a host of difficulties) the popular impressions are against me. But if I am honored with the same indulgent attention which the House has been pleased to afford me on past subjects of deliberation I do not despair of surmounting all these obstacles in the common cause of justice, humanity, and policy.

[1] Delivered in the Assembly of Maryland in 1788. A committee report favorable to the relief of slaves was then under consideration.

The report appears to me to have two objects in view: to annihilate the existing restraints on the voluntary emancipation of slaves, and to relieve a particular offspring from the punishment, heretofore inflicted on them, for the mere transgression of their parents. To the whole report, separately and collectively, my hearty assent, my cordial assistance, shall be given. It was the policy of this country, sir, from an early period of colonization, down to the Revolution, to encourage an importation of slaves for purposes which (if conjecture may be indulged) had been far better answered without their assistance. That this inhuman policy was a disgrace to the Colony, a dishonor to the Legislature, and a scandal to human nature, we need not at this enlightened period labor to prove.

The generous mind, that has adequate ideas of the inherent rights of mankind and knows the value of them, must feel its indignation rise against the shameful traffic that introduces slavery into a country which seems to have been designed by providence as an asylum for those whom the arm of power had persecuted and not as a nursery for wretches stripped of every privilege which heaven intended for its rational creatures, and reduced to a level with—nay, become themselves—the mere goods and chattels of their masters.

Sir, by the eternal principles of natural justice, no master in the State has a right to hold his slave in bondage for a single hour; but the law of the land, which (however oppressive and unjust, however inconsistent with the great groundwork of the late Revolution and our present frame of government) we can not in prudence or from a regard to individual rights abolish, has authorized a slavery as bad or perhaps worse than the most absolute, unconditional servitude that ever England knew in the early ages of its empire, under the tyrannical policy of the Danes, the feudal tenures of the Saxons, or the pure villanage of the Normans.

But, Mr. Speaker, because a respect for the peace and safety of the community, and the already injured rights of individuals, forbids a compulsory liberation of these unfortunate creatures, shall we unnecessarily refine upon this gloomy system of bondage and prevent the owner of a slave from manumitting him at the only probable period when the warm feelings of benevolence and the gentle workings of commiseration dispose him to the generous deed?

Sir, I sincerely wish it were in my power to impart my feelings upon this subject to those who hear me; they would then acknowledge that while the owner was protected in the property of his slave he might at the same time be allowed to relinquish that property to the unhappy subject whenever he should be so inclined. They would then feel that denying this privilege was repugnant to every principle of humanity—an everlasting stigma on our government—an act of unequaled barbarity, without a color of policy or a pretext of necessity to justify it.

Sir, let gentlemen put it home to themselves, that after providence has crowned our exertions in the cause of general freedom with success, and led us on to independence through a myriad of dangers and in defiance of obstacles crowding thick upon each other, we should not so soon forget the principles upon which we fled to arms and lose all sense of that interposition of heaven by which alone we could have been saved from the grasp of arbitrary power. We may talk of liberty in our public councils and fancy that we feel reverence for her dictates. We may declaim, with all the vehemence of animated rhetoric, against oppression, and flatter ourselves that we detest the ugly monster, but so long as we continue to cherish the poisonous weed of partial slavery among us the world will doubt our sincerity. In the name of heaven, with what face can we call ourselves the friends of equal freedom and the inherent rights of our species when we wantonly pass laws inimical to each; when we reject every opportunity of destroying, by silent, imperceptible degrees, the horrid fabric of individual bondage, reared by the mercenary hands of those from whom the sacred flame of liberty received no devotion?

Sir, it is pitiable to reflect to what wild inconsistencies, to what opposite extremes we are hurried by the frailty of our nature. Long have I been convinced that no generous sentiment of which the human heart is capable, no elevated passion of the soul that dignifies mankind, can obtain a uniform and perfect dominion: to-day we may be aroused as one man, by a wonderful and unaccountable sympathy against the lawless invader of the rights of his fellow creatures: to-morrow we may be guilty of the same oppression which we reprobated and resisted in another.

Is it, Mr. Speaker, because the complexion of these devoted victims is not quite so delicate as ours; is it because their untutored minds (humbled and debased by the hereditary yoke) appear less active and capricious than our own; or is it because we have been so habituated to their situation as to become callous to the horrors of it that we are determined, whether politic or not, to keep them till time shall be no more on a level with the brutes? For "nothing," says Montesquieu, "so much assimilates a man to a brute as living among freemen, himself a slave." Call not Maryland a land of liberty; do not pretend that she has chosen this country as an asylum, that here she has erected her temple and consecrated her shrine, when here, also, her unhallowed enemy holds his hellish pandemonium and our rulers offer sacrifice at his polluted altar. The lily and the bramble may grow in social proximity, but liberty and slavery delight in separation.

Sir, let us figure to ourselves for a moment

one of these unhappy victims, more informed than the rest, pleading at the bar of this House the cause of himself and his fellow sufferers; what would be the language of this orator of nature? Thus my imagination tells me he would address us:

"We belong by the policy of the country to our masters, and submit to our rigorous destiny; we do not ask you to divest them of their property, because we are conscious you have not the power; we do not entreat you to compel an emancipation of us or our posterity, because justice to your fellow citizens forbids it; we only supplicate you not to arrest the gentle arm of humanity when it may be stretched forth in our behalf; nor to wage hostilities against that moral or religious conviction which may at any time incline our masters to give freedom to us or our unoffending offspring; not to interpose legislative obstacles to the course of voluntary manumission.

"Thus shall you neither violate the rights of your people nor endanger the quiet of the community, while you vindicate your public councils from the imputation of cruelty and the stigma of causeless, unprovoked oppression. We have never," would he argue, "rebelled against our masters; we have never thrown your government into a ferment by struggles to regain the independence of our fathers. We have yielded our necks submissive to the yoke, and without a murmur acquiesced in the privation of our native rights. We conjure you, then, in the name of the common Parent of mankind, reward us not for this long and patient acquiescence by shutting up the main avenues to our liberation, by withholding from us the poor privilege of benefiting by the kind indulgence, the generous intentions of our superiors.''

What could we answer to arguments like these? Silent and peremptory, we might reject the application, but no words could justify the deed.

In vain should we resort to apologies grounded on the fallacious suggestions of a cautious and timid policy. I would as soon believe the incoherent tale of a schoolboy who should tell me he had been frightened by a ghost as that the grant of this permission ought in any degree to alarm us. Are we apprehensive that these men will become more dangerous by becoming free? Are we alarmed lest, by being admitted to the enjoyment of civil rights, they will be inspired with a deadly enmity against the rights of others? Strange, unaccountable paradox! How much more rational would it be to argue that the natural enemy of the privileges of freemen is he who is robbed of them himself! In him the foul demon of jealousy converts the sense of his own debasement into a rancorous hatred for the more auspicious fate of others; while from him whom you have raised from the degrading sit-

uation of a slave, whom you have restored to
that rank in the order of the universe which
the malignancy of his fortune prevented him
from attaining before, from such a man (unless his soul be ten thousand times blacker than
his complexion) you may reasonably hope for
all the happy effects of the warmest gratitude
and love.

Sir, let us not limit our views to the short
period of a life in being; let us extend them
along the continuous line of endless generations
yet to come. How will the millions that now
teem in the womb of futurity, and whom your
present laws would doom to the curse of perpetual bondage, feel the inspiration of gratitude to those whose sacred love of liberty shall
have opened the door to their admission within
the pale of freedom! Dishonorable to the
species is the idea that they would ever prove
injurious to our interests. Released from the
shackles of slavery by the justice of government and the bounty of individuals, the want
of fidelity and attachment would be next to
impossible.

Sir, when we talk of policy, it would be well
for us to reflect whether pride is not at the
bottom of it; whether we do not feel our vanity
and self-consequence wounded at the idea of a
dusky African participating equally with ourselves in the rights of human nature, and rising to a level with us from the lowest point of
degradation. Prejudices of this kind, sir, are

often so powerful as to persuade us that whatever countervails them is the extremity of folly and that the peculiar path of wisdom is that which leads to their gratification.

But it is for us to be superior to the influence of such ungenerous motives; it is for us to reflect that whatever the complexion, however ignoble the ancestry or uncultivated the mind, one universal Father gave being to them and us; and, with that being conferred the inalienable rights of the species. But I have heard it argued that if you permit a master to manumit his slaves by his last will and testament, as soon as they discover he has done so they will destroy him to prevent a revocation. Never was a weaker defense attempted to justify the severity of persecution; never did a bigoted inquisition condemn a heretic to torture and to death upon grounds less adequate to justify the horrid sentence. Sir, is it not obvious that the argument applies equally against all devices whatsoever for any person's benefit? For, if an advantageous bequest is made, even to a white man, has he not the same temptation to cut short the life of his benefactor to secure and accelerate the enjoyment of the benefit?

HAMILTON

ON THE ADOPTION OF THE FEDERAL CONSTITUTION [1]
(1788)

Born in 1757, died in 1804; a Pamphleteer in the agitation preceding the Revolution; a Captain of Artillery in 1776; on Washington's Staff in 1777-81; won distinction at Yorktown in 1781; Member of the Continental Congress in 1782; Member of the Constitutional Convention of 1787; Secretary of the Treasury in 1789; Commander-in-Chief of the army in 1799; killed in a duel by Aaron Burr in 1804.

I AM persuaded, Mr. Chairman, that I in my turn shall be indulged in addressing the committee. We all in equal sincerity profess to be anxious for the establishment of a republican government on a safe and solid basis. It is the object of the wishes of every honest man in the United States, and I presume that I shall not be disbelieved when I declare that it is an object of all others the nearest and most dear to my own heart. The means of accomplishing this great purpose become the most important study which can interest mankind. It is our duty to examine all those means with peculiar attention and to choose the best and most effectual. It is our duty to draw from nature, from reason, from examples, the best

[1] Delivered on June 24, 1788, in the New York Convention, called to ratify the Constitution of the United States.

principles of policy, and to pursue and apply them in the formation of our government. We should contemplate and compare the systems which in this examination come under our view; distinguish with a careful eye the defects and excellencies of each, and, discarding the former, incorporate the latter, as far as circumstances will admit, into our Constitution. If we pursue a different course and neglect this duty we shall probably disappoint the expectations of our country and of the world.

In the commencement of a revolution which received its birth from the usurpations of tyranny, nothing was more natural than that the public mind should be influenced by an extreme spirit of jealousy. To resist these encroachments and to nourish this spirit was the great object of all our public and private institutions. The zeal for liberty became predominant and excessive. In forming our Confederation this passion alone seemed to actuate us, and we appear to have had no other view than to secure ourselves from despotism. The object certainly was a valuable one, and deserved our utmost attention. But, sir, there is another object equally important and which our enthusiasm rendered us little capable of regarding; I mean a principle of strength and stability in the organization of our government, and vigor in its operations. This purpose can never be accomplished but by the establishment of some select body formed peculiarly upon this principle. There are few positions more demonstrable than that there should be in every republic some permanent body to correct the prejudices, check the intemperate passions, and regulate the fluctuations of a popular assembly. It is evident that a body instituted for these purposes must be so formed as to exclude as much as possible from its own character those infirmities and that mutability which it is designed to remedy. It is therefore necessary that it should be small, that it should hold its authority during a considerable period, and that it should have such an independence in the exercise of its powers as will divest it as much as possible of local prejudices. It should be so formed as to be the center of political knowledge, to pursue always a steady line of conduct, and to reduce every irregular propensity to system. Without this establishment we may make experiments without end, but shall never have an efficient government.

It is an unquestionable truth that the body of the people in every country desire sincerely its prosperity; but it is equally unquestionable that they do not possess the discernment and stability necessary for systematic government. To deny that they are frequently led into the grossest errors by misinformation and passion would be a flattery which their own good sense must despise. That branch of administration especially which involves our political relations with foreign States, a community will ever be incompetent to. These truths are not often held up in public assemblies, but they can not be unknown to any who hear me. From these principles it follows that there ought to be two distinct bodies in our government: one, which shall be immediately constituted by and peculiarly represent the people and possess all the popular features; another, formed upon the principle and for the purposes before explained. Such considerations as these induced the Convention who formed your State Constitution to institute a Senate upon the present plan. The history of ancient and modern republics had taught them that many of the evils which these republics had suffered arose from the want of a certain balance and mutual control indispensable to a wise administration. They were convinced that popular assemblies are frequently misguided by ignorance, by sudden impulses, and the intrigues of ambitious men, and that some firm barrier against these operations was necessary; they therefore instituted your Senate, and the benefits we have experienced have fully justified their conceptions.

Gentlemen in their reasoning have placed the interests of the several States and those of the United States in contrast; this is not a fair view of the subject: they must necessarily be involved in each other. What we apprehend is that some sinister prejudice or some prevailing passion may assume the form of a genuine interest. The influence of these is as powerful as the most permanent conviction of the public good, and against this influence we ought to provide. The local interests of a State ought in every case to give way to the interests of the Union; for when a sacrifice of one or the other is necessary, the former becomes only an apparent, partial interest, and should yield on the principle that the small good ought never to oppose the great one. When you assemble from your several counties in the Legislature, were every member to be guided only by the apparent interests of his county, government would be impracticable. There must be a perpetual accommodation and sacrifice of local advantages to general expediency; but the spirit of a mere popular assembly would rarely be actuated by this important principle. It is therefore absolutely necessary that the Senate should be so formed as to be unbiased by false conceptions of the real interests or undue attachment to the apparent good of their several States.

Gentlemen indulge too many unreasonable apprehensions of danger to the State governments; they seem to suppose that the moment you put men into a national council, they become corrupt and tyrannical and lose all their affection for their fellow citizens. But can we imagine that the Senators will ever be so insensible of their own advantage as to sacrifice the genuine interest of their constituents? The

State governments are essentially necessary to the form and spirit of the general system. As long, therefore, as Congress has a full conviction of this necessity, they must even upon principles purely national, have as firm an attachment to the one as to the other. This conviction can never leave them, unless they become madmen. While the Constitution continues to be read and its principle known the States must by every rational man be considered as essential, component parts of the Union; and therefore the idea of sacrificing the former to the latter is wholly inadmissible.

The objectors do not advert to the natural strength and resources of State governments, which will ever give them an important superiority over the general government. If we compare the nature of their different powers, or the means of popular influence which each possesses, we shall find the advantage entirely on the side of the States. This consideration, important as it is, seems to have been little attended to. The aggregate number of representatives throughout the States may be two thousand. Their personal influence will, therefore, be proportionably more extensive than that of one or two hundred men in Congress. The State establishments of civil and military officers of every description, infinitely surpassing in number any possible correspondent establishments in the general government, will create such an extent and complication of attachments as will ever secure the predilection and support of the people. Whenever, therefore, Congress shall meditate any infringement of the State Constitutions, the great body of the people will naturally take part with their domestic representatives. Can the general government withstand such a united opposition? Will the people suffer themselves to be stripped of their privileges? Will they suffer their Legislatures to be reduced to a shadow and a name? The idea is shocking to common sense.

From the circumstances already explained and many others which might be mentioned, results a complicated, irresistible check, which must ever support the existence and importance of the State governments. The danger, if any exists, flows from an opposite source. The probable evil is that the general government will be too dependent on the State Legislatures, too much governed by their prejudices, and too obsequious to their humors; that the States, with every power in their hands, will make encroachments on the national authority till the Union is weakened and dissolved.

Every member must have been struck with an observation of a gentleman from Albany. Do what you will, says he, local prejudices and opinions will go into the government. What! shall we then form a Constitution to cherish and strengthen these prejudices? Shall we confirm the distemper instead of remedying it? It is undeniable that there must be a control somewhere. Either the general interest is to control the particular interests, or the contrary. If the former, then certainly the government ought to be so framed as to render the power of control efficient to all intents and purposes; if the latter, a striking absurdity follows; the controlling powers must be as numerous as the varying interests, and the operations of the government must therefore cease; for the moment you accommodate these different interests, which is the only way to set the government in motion, you establish a controlling power. Thus, whatever constitutional provisions are made to the contrary, every government will be at last driven to the necessity of subjecting the partial to the universal interest. The gentlemen ought always in their reasoning to distinguish between the real, genuine good of a State and the opinions and prejudices which may prevail respecting it; the latter may be opposed to the general good, and consequently ought to be sacrificed; the former is so involved in it that it never can be sacrificed.

There are certain social principles in human nature from which we may draw the most solid conclusions with respect to the conduct of individuals and of communities. We love our families more than our neighbors; we love our neighbors more than our countrymen in general. The human affections, like the solar heat, lose their intensity as they depart from the center and become languid in proportion to the expansion of the circle on which they act. On these principles, the attachment of the individual will be first and for ever secured by the State governments; they will be a mutual protection and support. Another source of influence, which has already been pointed out, is the various official connections in the States. Gentlemen endeavor to evade the force of this by saying that these offices will be insignificant. This is by no means true. The State officers will ever be important, because they are necessary and useful. Their powers are such as are extremely interesting to the people; such as affect their property, their liberty, and life. What is more important than the administration of justice and the execution of the civil and criminal laws? Can the State governments become insignificant while they have the power of raising money independently and without control? If they are really useful, if they are calculated to promote the essential interests of the people, they must have their confidence and support. The States can never lose their powers till the whole people of America are robbed of their liberties. These must go together; they must support each other, or meet one common fate. On the gentleman's principle we may safely trust the State governments, tho we have no means of resisting them; but we can not confide in the national government, tho we have an effectual constitutional guard against every encroachment. This is the essence of their argu-

ment, and it is false and fallacious beyond conception.

With regard to the jurisdiction of the two
governments I shall certainly admit that the
Constitution ought to be so formed as not to
prevent the States from providing for their own
existence; and I maintain that it is so formed,
and that their power of providing for themselves is sufficiently established. This is conceded by one gentleman, and in the next breath
the concession is retracted. He says Congress
has but one exclusive right in taxation—that of
duties on imports; certainly, then, their other
powers are only concurrent. But to take off
the force of this obvious conclusion, he immediately says that the laws of the United States are
supreme and that where there is one supreme
there can not be a concurrent authority; and
further, that where the laws of the Union are
supreme those of the States must be subordinate,
because there can not be two supremes. This is
curious sophistry. That two supreme powers can
not act together is false. They are inconsistent
only when they are aimed at each other or at one
indivisible object. The laws of the United States
are supreme as to all their proper constitutional
objects; the laws of the States are supreme in the
same way. These supreme laws may act on different objects without clashing, or they may
operate on different parts of the same common
object with perfect harmony. Suppose both
governments should lay a tax of a penny on a

certain article; has not each an independent and uncontrollable power to collect its own tax? The meaning of the maxim, there can not be two supremes, is simply this—two powers can not be supreme over each other. This meaning is entirely perverted by the gentlemen. But, it is said, disputes between collectors are to be referred to the Federal courts. This is again wandering in the field of conjecture. But suppose the fact is certain, is it not to be presumed that they will express the true meaning of the Constitution and the laws? Will they not be bound to consider the concurrent jurisdiction; to declare that both the taxes shall have equal operation; that both the powers, in that respect, are sovereign and coextensive? If they transgress their duty we are to hope that they will be punished. Sir, we can reason from probabilities alone. When we leave common sense and give ourselves up to conjecture, there can be no certainty, no security in our reasonings.

MARSHALL

ON THE FEDERAL CONSTITUTION[1]

(1788)

Born in 1755, died in 1835; served in the army during the Revolution;
Member of the Virginia Ratifying Convention in 1788; made Envoy
to France in 1797; elected to Congress in 1799; Secretary of State in
1800; Chief Justice of the Supreme Court in 1801–35.

MR. CHAIRMAN, I conceive that the object of
the discussion now before us is whether democracy or despotism be most eligible. I am sure
that those who framed the system submitted to
our investigation, and those who now support
it, intend the establishment and security of the
former. The supporters of the Constitution
claim the title of being firm friends of the liberty and the rights of mankind. They say that
they consider it as the best means of protecting
liberty. We, sir, idolize democracy. Those who
oppose it have bestowed eulogiums on monarchy.
We prefer this system to any monarchy because
we are convinced that it has a greater tendency
to secure our liberty and promote our happiness. We admire it because we think it a well-
regulated democracy: it is recommended to the
good people of this country: they are, through

[1] Delivered on June 10, 1738, in the Virginia Convention called to
ratify the Constitution of the United States.

us, to declare whether it be such a plan of government as will establish and secure their freedom.

Permit me to attend to what the honorable gentleman, Mr. Henry,[1] has said. He has expatiated on the necessity of a due attention to certain maxims, to certain fundamental principles from which a free people ought never to depart. I concur with him in the propriety of the observance of such maxims. They are necessary in every government, but more essential to a democracy than to any other.

What are the favorite maxims of democracy? A strict observance of justice and public faith and a steady adherence to virtue. These, sir, are the principles of a good government. No mischief, no misfortune, ought to deter us from a strict observance of justice and public faith. Would to heaven that these principles had been observed under the present government! Had this been the case the friends of liberty would not be so willing now to part with it. Can we boast that our government is founded on these maxims? Can we pretend to the enjoyment of political freedom or security when we are told that a man has been, by an act of Assembly, struck out of existence without a trial by jury, without examination, without being confronted with his accusers and witnesses, without the benefits of the law of the land? Where is our

[1] Patrick Henry. See page 67 of this volume for his speech in the Virginia Convention.

safety when we are told that this act was justifiable because the person was not a Socrates? What has become of the worthy member's maxims? Is this one of them? Shall it be a maxim that a man shall be deprived of his life without the benefit of law? Shall such a deprivation of life be justified by answering that a man's life was not taken *secundem artem*, because he was a bad man? Shall it be a maxim that government ought not to be empowered to protect virtue?

The honorable member, after attempting to vindicate that tyrannical legislative act to which I have been alluding, proceeded to take a view of the dangers to which this country is exposed. He told us that the principal danger arose from a government which, if adopted, would give away the Mississippi.

I intended to proceed regularly by attending to the clause under debate; but I must reply to some observations which were dwelt upon to make impressions on our minds unfavorable to the plan upon the table. Have we no navigation in, or do we derive no benefit from, the Mississippi? How shall we retain it? By retaining that weak government which has hitherto kept it from us? Is it thus that we shall secure that navigation? Give the government the power of retaining it and then we may hope to derive actual advantages from it. Till we do this we can not expect that a government which hitherto has not been able to protect it will have the power to do it hereafter. Have we attended too long to consider whether this government would be able to protect us? Shall we wait for further proofs of its inefficacy? If on mature consideration the Constitution will be found to be perfectly right on the subject of treaties and containing no danger of losing that navigation, will he still object? Will he object because eight States are unwilling to part with it? This is no good ground of objection.

He then stated the necessity and probability of obtaining amendments. This we ought to postpone until we come to that clause, and make up our minds whether there be anything unsafe in this system. He conceived it impossible to obtain amendments after adopting it. If he was right, does not his own argument prove that in his own conception previous amendments can not be had? for, sir, if subsequent amendments can not be obtained, shall we get amendments before we ratify? The reasons against the latter do not apply against the former.

There are in this State, and in every State in the Union, many who are decided enemies of the Union. Reflect on the probable conduct of such men. What will they do? They will bring amendments which are local in their nature and which they know will not be accepted. What security have we that other States will not do the same? We are told that many in the States were violently opposed to it. They are more mindful of local interests. They will never propose such amendments as they think would be obtained.

Disunion will be their object. This will be attained by the proposal of unreasonable amendments. This, sir, tho a strong cause, is not the only one that will militate against previous amendments. Look at the comparative temper of this country now, and when the late Federal Convention met. We had no idea then of any particular system. The formation of the most perfect plan was our object and wish. It was imagined that the States would accede to and be pleased with the proposition that would be made them. Consider the violence of opinions, the prejudices, and animosities which have been since imbibed.

Will not these operate greatly against mutual concessions or a friendly concurrence? This will, however, be taken up more properly another time. He says we wish to have a strong, energetic, powerful government. We contend for a well-regulated democracy. He insinuates that the power of the government has been enlarged by the convention and that we may apprehend it will be enlarged by others. The convention did not, in fact, assume any power.

They have proposed to our consideration a scheme of government which they thought advisable. We are not bound to adopt it if we disapprove of it. Had not every individual in this community a right to tender that scheme which he thought most conducive to the welfare of his country? Have not several gentlemen already demonstrated that the Convention did not exceed their powers? But the Congress have the power of making bad laws, it seems. The Senate, with the president, he informs us, may make a treaty which shall be disadvantageous to us; and that, if they be not good men, it will not be a good constitution. I shall ask the worthy member only if the people at large, and they alone, ought to make laws and treaties. Has any man this in contemplation?

You can not exercise the powers of government personally yourselves. You must trust to agents. If so, will you dispute giving them the power of acting for you, from an existing possibility that they may abuse it? As long as it is impossible for you to transact your business in person, if you repose no confidence in delegates because there is a possibility of their abusing it, you can have no government.

The honorable gentleman has asked if there be any safety or freedom when we give away the sword and the purse. Shall the people at large hold the sword and the purse without the interposition of their representatives? Can the whole aggregate community act personally? I apprehend that every gentleman will see the impossibility of this. Must they, then, not trust them to others? To whom are they to trust them but to their representatives, who are accountable for their conduct?

He represents secrecy as unnecessary and produces the British government as a proof of its inutility. Is there no secrecy there? When deliberating on the propriety of declaring war, or on military arrangements, do they deliberate in the open fields?

No, sir. The British government affords secrecy when necessary, and so ought every government. In this plan, secrecy is only used when it would be fatal and pernicious to publish the schemes of government. We are threatened with the loss of our liberties by the possible abuse of power, notwithstanding the maxim that those who give may take away. It is the people that give power and can take it back. What shall restrain them? They are the masters who give it, and of whom their servants hold it.

He then argues against the system because it does not resemble the British government in this—that the same power that declares war has not the means of carrying it on. Are the people of England more secure if the Commons have no voice in declaring war? or are we less secure by having the Senate joined with the president? It is an absurdity, says the worthy member, that the same man should obey two masters, that the same collector should gather taxes for the general government and the State Legislature. Are they not both the servants of the people? Are not Congress and the State Legislature the agents of the people, and are they not to consult the good of the people? May this not be effected by giving the same officer the collection of both taxes? He tells you that it is an absurdity to adopt before you amend. Is the object of your adoption to amend solely? The objects of your adoption are union, safety against foreign enemies, and protection against faction—against what has been the destruction of all republics.

These impel you to its adoption. If you adopt it what shall restrain you from amending it if, in trying it, amendments shall be found necessary? The government is not supported by force, but depending on our free will. When experience shall show us any inconvenience we can then correct it. But until we have experience on the subject, amendments as well as the Constitution itself are to be tried.

Let us try it and keep our hands free to change it when necessary. If it be necessary to change government, let us change that government which has been found to be defective. The difficulty we find in amending the confederation will not be found in amending this Constitution.

Any amendments in the system before you will not go to a radical change; a plain way is pointed out for the purpose. All will be interested to change it, and therefore all exert themselves in getting the change. There is such a diversity of sentiment in human minds that it is impossible we shall ever concur in one system till we try it. The power given to the general government over the time, place, and manner of election is also strongly objected to. When we come to that clause we can prove it is highly necessary and not dangerous.

The worthy member has concluded his observations by many eulogiums on the British Constitution. It matters not to us whether it be a wise one or not. I think that, for America at least, the government on your table is very much superior to it. I ask you if your House of Representatives would be better than it is if a hundredth part of the people were to elect a majority of them. If your senators were for life, would they be more agreeable to you? If your president were not accountable to you for his conduct—if it were a constitutional maxim that he could do no wrong—would you be safer than you are now?

If you can answer "Yes" to these questions, then adopt the British Constitution. If not, then good as that government may be, this is better. The worthy gentleman who was last up said the confederacies of ancient and modern times were not similar to ours, and that consequently reasons which applied against them could not be urged against it. Do they not hold out one lesson very useful to us? However unlike in other respects, they resemble it in its total inefficacy. They warn us to shun their calamities, and place in our government those necessary powers the want of which destroyed them. I hope we shall avail ourselves of their misfortunes without experiencing them. There was something peculiar in one observation he made. He said that those who governed the cantons of Switzerland were purchased by foreign powers, which was the cause of their uneasiness and trouble. How does this apply to us? If we adopt such a government as theirs, will it not be subject to the same inconvenience? Will not the same cause produce the same effect? What shall protect us from it? What is our security?

He then proceeded to say the causes of war are removed from us; that we are separated by the sea from the powers of Europe and need not be alarmed. Sir, the sea makes them neighbors to us. Tho an immense ocean divides us we may speedily see them with us. What dangers may we not apprehend to our commerce! Does not our naval weakness invite an attack on our commerce? May not the Algerines seize our vessels? Can not they and every other predatory or maritime nation pillage our ships and destroy our commerce without subjecting themselves to any inconvenience?

He would, he said, give the general government all necessary powers. If anything be necessary it must be so to call forth the strength of the Union when we may be attacked or when the general purposes of America require it. The worthy gentleman then proceeded to show that our present exigencies are greater than they will ever be again.

Who can penetrate into futurity? How can

any man pretend to say that our future exigencies will be less than our present? The exigencies of nations have been generally commensurate to their resources. It would be the utmost impolicy to trust to a mere possibility of not being attacked or obliged to exert the strength of the community. He then spoke of a selection of particular objects by Congress which he says must necessarily be oppressive; that Congress, for instance, might select taxes and that all but landholders would escape. Can not Congress regulate the taxes so as to be equal on all parts of the community? Where is the absurdity of having thirteen revenues? Will they clash with or injure each other? If not, why can not Congress make thirteen distinct laws and impose the taxes on the general objects of taxation in each State so that all persons of society shall pay equally, as they ought?

He then told you that your continental government will call forth the virtue and talents of America. This being the case, will they encroach on the power of the State governments? Will our most virtuous and able citizens wantonly attempt to destroy the liberty of the people? Will the most virtuous act the most wickedly? I differ in opinion from the worthy gentleman. I think the virtue and talents of the members of the general government will tend to the security instead of the destruction of our liberty. I think that the power of direct taxation is essential to the existence of the general government and that it is safe to grant it. If this power be not necessary, and as safe from abuse as any delegated power can possibly be, then I say that the plan before you is unnecessary, for it imports not what system we have, unless it have the power of protecting us in time of peace and war.

FISHER AMES

ON THE TREATY WITH GREAT BRITAIN[1]
(1796)

Born in 1758, died in 1808; member of the Massachusetts Ratifying
Committee in 1788; Member of Congress in 1789; declined the
Presidency of Harvard College in 1804.

It would be strange that a subject which has
aroused in turn all the passions of the country
should be discussed without the interference
of any of our own. We are men, and, therefore, not exempt from those passions; as citizens and representatives we feel the interests
that must excite them. The hazard of great interests can not fail to agitate strong passions.
We are not disinterested; it is impossible we
should be dispassionate. The warmth of such
feelings may becloud the judgment and for a
time pervert the understanding. But the public sensibility, and our own, has sharpened the
spirit of inquiry and given an animation to the
debate. The public attention has been quick-

[1] Delivered in the House of Representatives on April 28, 1796.
On November 19, 1794, a "treaty of amity, commerce, and navigation" with Great Britain had been concluded, and in March, 1796, was
proclaimed as the law of the land. On April 28 a resolution was
offered that it would be expedient "to pass the laws necessary for
carrying the treaty into effect." Mr. Ames's speech was on this
resolution. Abridged.

ened to mark the progress of the discussion, and its judgment, often hasty and erroneous on first impressions, has become solid and enlightened at last. Our result will, I hope, on that account be safer and more mature, as well as more accordant with that of the nation. The only constant agents in political affairs are the passions of men. Shall we complain of our nature—shall we say that man ought to have been made otherwise? It is right already, because He, from whom we derive our nature, ordained it so; and because thus made and thus acting, the cause of truth and the public good is more surely promoted.

The treaty is bad, fatally bad, is the cry. It sacrifices the interest, the honor, the independence of the United States and the faith of our engagements to France. If we listen to the clamor of party intemperance, the evils are of a number not to be counted, and of a nature not to be borne, even in idea. The language of passion and exaggeration may silence that of sober reason in other places; it has not done it here. The question here is, whether the treaty be really so very fatal as to oblige the nation to break its faith. I admit that such a treaty ought not to be executed. I admit that self-preservation is the first law of society as well as of individuals. It would, perhaps, be deemed an abuse of terms to call that a treaty which violates such a principle. I waive, also, for the present, any inquiry what departments shall represent the nation and annul the stipulations of a treaty.

I content myself with pursuing the inquiry whether the nature of this compact be such as to justify our refusal to carry it into effect. A treaty is the promise of a nation. Now, promises do not always bind him that makes them. But I lay down two rules which ought to guide us in this case. The treaty must appear to be bad, not merely in the petty details, but in its character, principle, and mass. And in the next place, this ought to be ascertained by the decided and general concurrence of the enlightened public.

I confess there seems to be something very like ridicule thrown over the debate by the discussion of the articles in detail. The undecided point is, shall we break our faith? And while our country and enlightened Europe await the issue with more than curiosity, we are employed to gather piecemeal, and article by article, from the instrument, a justification for the deed by trivial calculations of commercial profit and loss. This is little worthy of the subject of this body, or of the nation. If the treaty is bad it will appear to be so in its mass. Evil to a fatal extreme, if that be its tendency, requires no proof; it brings it. Extremes speak for themselves and make their own law. What if the direct voyage of American ships to Jamaica with horses or lumber might net one or two *per centum* more than the present trade to Surinam; would the proof of the fact avail anything in so grave a question as the violation of the public engagements?

What is patriotism? Is it a narrow affection for the spot where a man was born? Are the very clods where we tread entitled to this ardent preference because they are greener? No, sir, this is not the character of the virtue, and it soars higher for its object. It is an extended self-love, mingling with all the enjoyments of life, and twisting itself with the minutest filaments of the heart. It is thus we obey the laws of society, because they are the laws of virtue. In their authority we see not the array of force and terror, but the venerable image of our country's honor. Every good citizen makes that honor his own and cherishes it not only as precious, but as sacred. He is willing to risk his life in its defense, and is conscious that he gains protection while he gives it. For, what rights of a citizen will be deemed inviolable when a State renounces the principles that constitute their security? Or if his life should not be invaded, what would its enjoyments be in a country odious in the eyes of strangers and dishonored in his own? Could he look with affection and veneration to such a country as his parent? The sense of having one would die within him; he would blush for his patriotism, if he retained any, and justly, for it would be a vice. He would be a banished man in his native land.

I see no exception to the respect that is paid among nations to the law of good faith. If there are cases in this enlightened period when it is violated, there are none when it is decried. It is the philosophy of politics, the religion of governments. It is observed by barbarians—a whiff of tobacco smoke, or a string of beads gives not merely binding force but sanctity to treaties. Even in Algiers a truce may be bought for money, but when ratified even Algiers is too wise, or too just, to disown and annul its obligation. Thus we see, neither the ignorance of savages, nor the principles of an association for piracy and rapine, permit a nation to despise its engagements. If, sir, there could be a resurrection from the foot of the gallows, if the victims of justice could live again, collect together and form a society, they would, however loath, soon find themselves obliged to make justice that justice under which they fell, the fundamental law of their State. They would perceive it was their interest to make others respect, and they would, therefore, soon pay some respect themselves to the obligations of good faith.

It is painful, I hope it is superfluous, to make even the supposition that America should furnish the occasion of this opprobrium. No, let me not even imagine that a republican government, sprung as our own is from a people enlightened and uncorrupted, a government whose origin is right, and whose daily discipline is duty, can, upon solemn debate, make its option to be faithless—can dare to act what despots dare not avow, what our own example evinces, the States of Barbary are unsuspected of.

No, let me rather make the supposition that Great Britain refuses to execute the treaty, after we have done everything to carry it into effect. Is there any language of reproach pungent enough to express your commentary of the fact? What would you say, or, rather, what could you not say? Would you not tell them, wherever an Englishman might travel, shame would stick to him—he would disown his country. You would exclaim: England, proud of your wealth, and arrogant in the possession of power—blush for these distinctions which become the vehicles of your dishonor. Such a nation might truly say to corruption, thou art my father, and to the worm, thou are my mother and my sister. We would say of such a race of men, their name is a heavier burden than their debt.

On this theme my emotions are unutterable. If I could find words for them, if my powers bore any proportion of my zeal, I would swell my voice to such a note of remonstrance it should reach every log house beyond the mountains. I would say to the inhabitants: wake from your false security; your cruel dangers, your more cruel apprehensions are soon to be renewed; the wounds, yet unhealed, are to be torn open again; in the daytime your path through the woods will be ambushed; the darkness of midnight will glitter with the blaze of your dwellings. You are a father—the blood of your sons shall fatten your cornfield; you are a mother—the war-whoop shall wake the sleep of the cradle.

On this subject you need not suspect any deception on your feelings. It is a spectacle of horror which can not be overdrawn. If you have nature in your hearts, it will speak a language compared with which all I have said or can say will be poor and frigid.

Will it be whispered that the treaty has made me a new champion for the protection of the frontiers? It is known that my voice as well as my vote have been uniformly given in conformity with the ideas I have expressed. Protection is the right of the frontiers; it is our duty to give it.

Who will accuse me of wandering out of the subject? Who will say that I exaggerate the tendencies of our measures? Will any one answer by a sneer that all this is idle preaching? Will anyone deny that we are bound, and I would hope to good purpose, by the most solemn sanctions of duty for the vote we give? Are despots alone to be reproached for unfeeling indifference to the tears and blood of their subjects? Have the principles on which you ground the reproach upon cabinets and kings no practical influence, no binding force? Are they merely themes of idle declamation introduced to decorate the morality of a newspaper essay or to furnish petty topics of harang from the windows of that State House? I trust it is neither too presumptuous nor too late to ask. Can you put the dearest interest of society at risk without guilt and without remorse?

By rejecting the posts we light the savage fires—we bind the victims. This day we undertake to render account to the widows and orphans whom our decision will make, to the wretches that will be roasted at the stake, to our country, and I do not deem it too serious to say, to conscience and to God. We are answerable, and if duty be anything more than a word of imposture, if conscience be not a bugbear, we are preparing to make ourselves as wretched as our country.

There is no mistake in this case—there can be none. Experience has already been the prophet of events, and the cries of future victims have already reached us. The Western inhabitants are not a silent and uncomplaining sacrifice. The voice of humanity issues from the shade of their wilderness. It exclaims that, while one hand is held up to reject this treaty, the other grasps a tomahawk. It summons our imagination to the scenes that will open. It is no great effort of the imagination to conceive that events so near are already begun. I can fancy that I listen to the yells of savage vengeance and the shrieks of torture. Already they seem to sigh in the west wind—already they mingle with every echo from the mountains.

Let me cheer the mind, weary, no doubt, and ready to despond on this prospect, by presenting another, which it is yet in our power to realize. Is it possible for a real American to look at the prosperity of this country without some desire for its continuance—without some respect for the measures which, many will say, produce, and all will confess, have preserved it? Will he not feel some dread that a change of system will reverse the scene? The well-grounded fears of our citizens in 1794 were removed by the treaty, but are not forgotten. Then they deemed war nearly inevitable, and would not this adjustment have been considered at that day as a happy escape from the calamity? The great interest and the general desire of our people were to enjoy the advantages of neutrality. This instrument, however misrepresented, affords America that inestimable security. The causes of our disputes are either cut up by the roots or referred to a new negotiation after the end of the European war. This was gaining everything, because it confirmed our neutrality by which our citizens are gaining everything. This alone would justify the engagements of the government. For, when the fiery vapors of the war lowered in the skirts of our horizon, all our wishes were concentrated in this one, that we might escape the desolation of the storm. This treaty, like a rainbow on the edge of the cloud, marked to our eyes the space where it was raging and afforded at the same time the sure prognostic of fair weather. If we reject it the vivid colors will grow pale—it will be a baleful meteor portending tempest and war.

I rose to speak under the impressions that I would have resisted if I could. Those who see me will believe that the reduced state of my health has unfitted me almost equally for much exertion of body or mind. Unprepared for debate, by careful reflection in my retirement or by long attention here, I thought the resolution I had taken to sit silent was imposed by necessity, and would cost me no effort to maintain. With a mind thus vacant of ideas and sinking, as I really am, under a sense of weakness, I imagined the very desire of speaking was extinguished by the persuasion that I had nothing to say. Yet, when I come to the moment of deciding the vote I start back with dread from the edge of the pit into which we are plunging. In my view even the minutes I have spent in expostulation have their value, because they protract the crisis and the short period in which alone we may resolve to escape it.

I have thus been led by my feelings to speak more at length than I intended. Yet I have, perhaps, as little personal interest in the event as any one here. There is, I believe, no member who will not think his chance to be a witness of the consequences greater than mine. If,

however, the vote shall pass to reject, and a
spirit should rise, as it will, with the public
disorders, to make confusion worse confounded,
even I, slender and almost broken as my hold
upon life is, may outlive the government and
Constitution of my country.

JEFFERSON

HIS FIRST INAUGURAL ADDRESS [1]
(1801)

Born in 1743, died in 1826; Member of the Virginia House of Burgesses in 1769–75, and again in 1776–78; Member of the Continental Congress in 1775; drafted the Declaration of Independence in 1776; Governor of Virginia in 1779; Member of Congress in 1783; Minister to France in 1785; Secretary of State in 1790; Vice-President in 1797; elected President in 1801 and reelected in 1805.

CALLED upon to undertake the duties of the first executive office of our country, I avail myself of the presence of that portion of my fellow citizens which is here assembled, to express my grateful thanks for the favor with which they have been pleased to look toward me, to declare a sincere consciousness that the task is above my talents, and that I approach it with those anxious and awful presentiments which the greatness of the charge and the weakness of my powers so justly inspire.

A rising nation spread over a wide and fruitful land, traversing all the seas with the rich productions of their industry, engaged in commerce with nations who feel power and forget right, ad-

[1] Delivered in Washington on March 4, 1801. Jefferson went to the Capitol on horseback, in studiously plain clothes, and, having tied his horse to a fence, walked unceremoniously into the Senate-chamber, where he took the oath and delivered this speech.

vancing rapidly to destinies beyond the reach of mortal eye,—when I contemplate these transcendent objects, and see the honor, the happiness, and the hopes of this beloved country committed to the issue and the auspices of this day, I shrink from the contemplation, and humble myself before the magnitude of the undertaking. Utterly, indeed, should I despair, did not the presence of many whom I here see remind me that in the other high authorities provided by our Constitution I shall find resources of wisdom, of virtue, and of zeal on which to rely under all difficulties. To you, then, gentlemen, who are charged with the sovereign functions of legislation, and to those associated with you, I look with encouragement for that guidance and support which may enable us to steer with safety the vessel in which we are all embarked, amid the conflicting elements of a troubled world.

During the contest of opinion through which we have passed, the animation of discussions and of exertions has sometimes worn an aspect which might impose on strangers unused to think freely and to speak and to write what they think; but this being now decided by the voice of the nation, announced according to the rules of the Constitution, all will, of course, arrange themselves under the will of the law, and unite in common efforts for the common good. All, too, will bear in mind this sacred principle, that tho the will of the majority is in all cases to prevail, that will, to be rightful, must be reasonable; that the minority possess their equal rights, which equal law must protect, and to violate would be oppression.

Let us then, fellow citizens, unite with one heart and one mind; let us restore to social intercourse that harmony and affection without which liberty, and even life itself, are but dreary things. And let us reflect that, having banished from our land that religious intolerance under which mankind so long bled and suffered, we have yet gained little, if we countenance a political intolerance as despotic, as wicked, and capable of as bitter and bloody persecutions. During the throes and convulsions of the ancient world, during the agonizing spasms of infuriated man, seeking through blood and slaughter his long-lost liberty, it was not wonderful that the agitation of the billows should reach even this distant and peaceful shore; that this should be more felt and feared by some and less by others, and should divide opinions as to measures of safety; but every difference of opinion is not a difference of principle.

We have called by different names brethren of the same principle. We are all Republicans; we are all Federalists. If there be any among us who would wish to dissolve this Union, or to change its republican form, let them stand undisturbed as monuments of the safety with which error of opinion may be tolerated, where reason is left free to combat it. I know, indeed, that some honest men fear that a republican government can not be strong; that this government is not strong enough. But would the honest patriot, in the full tide of successful experiment, abandon a government which has so far kept us free and firm, on the theoretic and visionary fear that this government, the world's best hope, may, by possibility, want energy to preserve itself? I trust not. I believe this, on the contrary, the strongest government on earth. I believe it the only one where every man, at the call of the law, would fly to the standard of the law, and would meet invasions of the public order as his own personal concern. Sometimes it is said that man can not be trusted with the government of himself. Can he, then, be trusted with the government of others? Or have we found angels in the form of kings to govern him? Let history answer this question.

Let us, then, with courage and confidence, pursue our own federal and republican principles; our attachment to union and representative government. Kindly separated by nature and a wide ocean from the exterminating havoc of one-quarter of the globe; too high-minded to endure the degradations of the others; possessing a chosen country, with room enough for our descendants to the hundredth and thousandth generation; entertaining a due sense of our equal right to the use of our own facul-

ties, to the acquisitions of our own industry, to
honor and confidence from our fellow citizens,
resulting not from birth, but from our actions
and their sense of them; enlightened by a benign religion, professed, indeed, and practised
in various forms, yet all of them inculcating
honesty, truth, temperance, gratitude, and the
love of man, acknowledging and adoring an
overruling providence, which by all its dispen-
sations, proves that it delights in the happiness of man here and his greater happiness
hereafter; with all these blessings, what more is
necessary to make us a happy and a prosperous people?

Still one thing more, fellow citizens—a wise
and frugal government, which shall restrain
men from injuring one another, shall leave
them otherwise free to regulate their own pursuits of industry and improvement, and shall
not take from the mouth of labor the bread it
has earned. This is the sum of good government; and this is necessary to close the circle
of our felicities.

About to enter, fellow citizens, on the exercise of duties which comprehend everything
dear and valuable to you, it is proper you
should understand what I deem the essential
principles of our government, and consequently
those which ought to shape its administration.
I will compress them within the narrowest
compass they will bear, stating the general principle, but not all its limitations. Equal and

exact justice to all men, of whatever state or persuasion, religious or political; peace, commerce, and honest friendship with all nations, entangling alliances with none; the support of the State governments in all their rights, as the most competent administrations for our domestic concerns, and the surest bulwarks against antirepublican tendencies; the preservation of the general government in its whole constitutional vigor, as the sheet-anchor of our peace at home and safety abroad; a jealous care of the right of election by the people; a mild and safe corrective of abuses which are lopped by the sword of revolution, where peaceable remedies are unprovided; absolute acquiescence in the decisions of the majority, the vital principle of republics, from which is no appeal but to force, the vital principle and immediate parent of despotism; a well-disciplined militia, our best reliance in peace and for the first moments of war, till regulars may relieve them; the supremacy of the civil over the military authority; economy in the public expense, that labor may be lightly burdened; the honest payment of our debts, and sacred preservation of the public faith; encouragement of agriculture, and of commerce as its handmaid; the diffusion of information and arraignment of all abuses at the bar of the public reason; freedom of religion, freedom of the Press, and freedom of person, under the protection of the Habeas Corpus; and trial by juries impartially selected.

These principles form the bright constellation which has gone before us, and guided our steps through an age of revolution and reformation. The wisdom of our sages and blood of our heroes have been devoted to their attainment; they should be the creed of our political faith, the text of civic instruction, the touchstone by which to try the services of those we trust; and should we wander from them in moments of error or of alarm, let us hasten to retrace our steps and to regain the road which alone leads to peace, liberty, and safety.

I repair then, fellow citizens, to the post you have assigned me. With experience enough in subordinate offices to have seen the difficulties of this, the greatest of all, I have learned to expect that it will rarely fall to the lot of imperfect man to retire from this station with the reputation and the favor which bring him into it. Without pretensions to that high confidence you reposed in our first and greatest revolutionary character, whose preeminent services had entitled him to the first place in his country's love, and destined for him the fairest page in the volume of faithful history, I ask so much confidence only as may give firmness and effect to the legal administration of your affairs.

I shall often go wrong through defect of judgment. When right, I shall often be thought wrong by those whose positions will not command a view of the whole ground. I ask your indulgence for my own errors, which will never be intentional; and your support against the errors of others, who may condemn what they would not, if seen in all its parts. The approbation implied by your suffrage is a great consolation to me for the past; and my future solicitude will be to retain the good opinion of those who have bestowed it in advance, to conciliate that of others by doing them all the good in my power, and to be instrumental to the happiness and freedom of all.

Relying, then, on the patronage of your good will, I advance with obedience to the work, ready to retire from it whenever you become sensible how much better choices it is in your power to make. And may that Infinite Power which rules the destinies of the universe lead our councils to what is best, and give them a favorable issue for your peace and prosperity.

ELIPHALET NOTT

ON THE DEATH OF HAMILTON [1]

(1804)

Born in 1773, died in 1866; for a few years Pastor of Presbyterian
churches; made President of Union College, Schenectady, in 1804,
filling the place until 1866.

BEFORE such an audience and on such an occasion I enter on the duty assigned me with
trembling. Do not mistake my meaning. I
tremble indeed—not, however, through fear of
failing to merit your applause, for what have I
to do with that when addressing the dying and
treading on the ashes of the dead; not through
fear of failing justly to portray the character
of that great man who is at once the theme of
my encomium and regret. He needs not eulogy.
His work is finished, and death has removed
him beyond my censure, and I would fondly
hope, through grace, above my praise.

You will ask then why I tremble? I tremble
to think that I am called to attack, from this
place, a crime, the very idea of which almost

---

[1] From a sermon delivered in Albany on July 9, 1804—one of several sermons delivered by prominent preachers at that time, and
having for their immediate purpose the breaking up of the custom
of dueling. Doctor Nott's sermon was the most notable of the series.
It was widely read and exerted much influence. Parts of it have
long been familiar as a declamation for schoolboys.

freezes one with horror—a crime, too, which exists among the polite and polished orders of society, and which is accompanied with every aggravation; committed with cool deliberation, and openly in the face of day! But I have a duty to perform: and difficult and awful as that duty is, I will not shrink from it.

Would to God my talents were adequate to the occasion. But such as they are, I devoutly proffer them to unfold the nature and counteract the influence of that barbarous custom which, like a resistless torrent, is undermining the foundations of civil government, breaking down the barriers of social happiness, and sweeping away virtue, talents, and domestic felicity in its desolating course. Another and an illustrious character—a father—a general—a statesman—the very man who stood on an eminence and without a rival among sages and heroes, the future hope of his country in danger—this man, yielding to the influence of a custom which deserves our eternal reprobation, has been brought to an untimely end.

The Hero, called from his sequestered retreat, whose first appearance in the field, tho a stripling, conciliated the esteem of Washington, our good old father. Moving by whose side, during all the perils of the Revolution, our young chieftain was a contributor to the veteran's glory, the guardian of his person, and the copartner of his toils.

The Conqueror, who, sparing of human blood

when victory favored, stayed the uplifted arm
and nobly said to the vanquished enemy,
"Live!"

The Statesman, the correctness of whose principles and the strength of whose mind are inscribed on the records of Congress and on the
annals of the council chamber; whose genius
impressed itself upon the Constitution of his
country; and whose memory the government—
illustrious fabric, resting on this basis—will
perpetuate while it lasts; and shaken by the
violence of party should it fall, which may
Heaven avert, his prophetic declarations will be
found inscribed on its ruins.

The Counselor, who was at once the pride of
the bar and the admiration of the court; whose
apprehensions were quick as lightning, and
whose development of truth was luminous as its
path; whose argument no change of circumstances could embarrass; whose knowledge appeared intuitive; and who, by a single glance,
and with as much facility as the eye of the
eagle passes over the landscape, surveyed the
whole field of controversy; saw in what way
truth might be most successfully defended and
how error must be approached; and who, without ever stopping, ever hesitating, by a rapid
and manly march, led the listening judge and
the fascinated juror, step by step, through a
delightsome region, brightening as he advanced,
till his argument rose to demonstration, and
eloquence was rendered useless by conviction;

whose talents were employed on the side of righteousness; whose voice, whether in the council chamber, or at the bar of justice, was virtue's consolation; at whose approach oppressed humanity felt a secret rapture, and the heart of injured innocence leaped for joy.

Where Hamilton was, in whatever sphere he moved, the friendless had a friend, the fatherless a father, and the poor man, tho unable to reward his kindness, found an advocate. It was when the rich oppressed the poor; when the powerful menaced the defenseless; when truth was disregarded or the eternal principles of justice violated—it was on these occasions that he exerted all his strength; it was on these occasions that he sometimes soared so high and shone with a radiance so transcendent, I had almost said, so "heavenly, as filled those around him with awe and gave to him the force and authority of a prophet."

The Patriot, whose integrity baffled the scrutiny of inquisition; whose manly virtue never shaped itself to circumstances; who, always great, always himself, stood amid the varying tides of party, firm, like the rock which, far from land, lifts its majestic top above the waves and remains unshaken by the storms which agitate the ocean.

The Friend, who knew no guile; whose bosom was transparent and deep; in the bottom of whose heart was rooted every tender and sympathetic virtue; whose various worth opposing parties acknowledged while alive, and on whose tomb they unite, with equal sympathy and grief, to heap their honors.

I know he had his failings. I see, on the picture of his life—a picture rendered awful by greatness, and luminous by virtue—some dark shades. On these let the tear that pities human weakness fall; on these let the veil which covers human frailty rest. As a hero, as a statesman, as a patriot, he lived nobly: and would to God I could add, he nobly fell. Unwilling to admit his error in this respect, I go back to the period of discussion. I see him resisting the threatened interview. I imagine myself present in his chamber. Various reasons, for a time, seem to hold his determination in arrest. Various and moving objects pass before him and speak a dissuasive language. His country, which may need his counsels to guide, and his arm to defend, utters her veto. The partner of his youth, already covered with weeds, and whose tears flow down into her bosom, intercedes! His babes, stretching out their little hands and pointing to a weeping mother, with lisping eloquence, but eloquence which reaches a parent's heart, cry out, "Stay, stay, dear papa, ard live for us!"

But I have said, and I repeat it, there are those whom I can not forgive. I can not forgive that minister at the altar who has hitherto forborne to remonstrate on this subject. I can not forgive that public prosecutor who, entrusted with the duty of avenging his country's wrongs, has seen those wrongs, and taken no measures to avenge them. I can not forgive that judge upon the bench, or that governor in the chair of state, who has lightly passed over such offenses. I can not forgive the public, in whose opinion the duelist finds a sanctuary. I can not forgive you, my brethren, who till this late hour have been silent while successive murders were committed.

No; I can not forgive you that you have not in common with the freemen of this State, raised your voice to the powers that be and loudly and explicitly demanded an execution of your laws; demanded this in a manner which, if it did not reach the ear of government, would at least have reached the heavens and pleaded your excuse before the God that filleth them—in whose presence as I stand I should not feel myself innocent of the blood that crieth against us had I been silent. But I have not been silent. Many of you who hear me are my witnesses—the walls of yonder temple, where I have heretofore addressed you, are my witnesses, how freely I have animadverted upon this subject in the presence both of those who have violated the laws and of those whose indispensable duty it is to see the laws executed on those who violate them.

A short time since, and he who is the occasion of our sorrows was the ornament of his country. He stood on an eminence, and glory covered him. From that eminence he has fallen—suddenly, for ever fallen. His intercourse with the living world is now ended; and those who would hereafter find him must seek him in the grave. There, cold and lifeless, is the heart which just now was the seat of friendship. There, dim and sightless, is the eye whose radiant and enlivening orb beamed with intelligence; and there, closed for ever, are those lips on whose persuasive accents we have so often and so lately hung with transport! From the darkness which rests upon his tomb there proceeds, methinks, a light in which it is clearly seen that those gaudy objects which men pursue are only phantoms. In this light, how dimly shines the splendor of victory; how humble appears the majesty of grandeur! The bubble which seemed to have so much solidity has burst; and we again see that all below the sun is vanity.

True, the funeral eulogy has been pronounced; the sad and solemn procession has moved; the badge of mourning has already been decreed, and presently the sculptured marble will lift up its front, proud to perpetuate the name of Hamilton and rehearse to the passing traveler his virtues. Just tributes of respect! And to the living, useful. But to him, moldering in the narrow and humble habitation, what are they? How vain! how unavailing!

Approach, and behold while I lift from his sepulcher its covering! Ye admirers of his greatness, ye emulous of his talents and his fame, approach, and behold him now. How pale! How silent! No martial bands admire the adroitness of his movements; no fascinating throng weep, and melt, and tremble at his eloquence! Amazing change! A shroud! a coffin! a narrow, subterraneous cabin! This is all that now remains of Hamilton! And is this all that remains of him? During a life so transitory, what lasting monument, then, can our fondest hopes erect!

My brethren! we stand on the borders of an awful gulf, which is swallowing up all things human. And is there, amid this universal wreck, nothing stable, nothing abiding, nothing immortal, on which poor, frail, dying man can fasten? Ask the hero, ask the statesman, whose wisdom you have been accustomed to revere, and he will tell you. He will tell you, did I say? He has already told you from his death-bed, and his illumined spirit still whispers from the heavens, with well-known eloquence, the solemn admonition: "Mortals! hastening to the tomb, and once the companions of my pilgrimage, take warning and avoid my errors; cultivate the virtues I have recommended; choose the Savior I have chosen; live disinterestedly; live for immortality; and, would you rescue anything from final dissolution, lay it up in God."

Thus speaks, methinks, our deceased benefactor, and thus he acted during his last sad hours.

To the exclusion of every other concern, religion now claims all his thoughts. Disburdened of his sorrows, and looking up to God, he exclaims: "Grace, rich grace!" "I have," said he, clasping his dying hands, and with faltering tongue, "I have a tender reliance on the mercy of God in Christ." In token of this reliance, and as an expression of his faith, he receives the holy sacrament; and having done this, his mind becomes tranquil and serene. Thus he remains, thoughtful indeed, but unruffled to the last, and meets death with an air of dignified composure and with an eye directed to the heavens.

This last act, more than any other, sheds glory on his character. Everything else death effaces. Religion alone abides with him on his death-bed. He dies a Christian. This is all which can be enrolled of him among the archives of eternity. This is all that can make his name great in heaven. Let not the sneering infidel persuade you that this last act of homage to the Savior resulted from an enfeebled state of mental faculties or from perturbation occasioned by the near approach of death. No; his opinions concerning the divine mission of Jesus Christ and the validity of the holy Scriptures had long been settled, and settled after laborious investigation and extensive and deep research. These opinions were not concealed. I knew them myself. Some of you, who hear me, knew them; and had his life been spared it was his determination to have published them to the world, together with the facts and reasons on which they were founded.

Who was it that, overleaping the narrow bounds which had hitherto been set to the human mind, ranged abroad through the immensity of space, discovered and illustrated those laws by which the Deity unites, binds, and governs all things? Who was it, soaring into the sublime of astronomic science, numbered the stars of heaven, measured their spheres, and called them by their names? It was Newton. But Newton was a Christian. Newton, great as he was, received instruction from the lips and laid his honors at the feet of Jesus. Who was it that developed the hidden combination, the component parts of bodies? Who was it dissected the animal, examined the flower, penetrated the earth, and ranged the extent of organic nature? It was Boyle. But Boyle was a Christian. Who was it that lifted the veil which had for ages covered the intellectual world, analyzed the human mind, defined its powers, and reduced its operations to certain and fixed laws? It was Locke. But Locke, too, was a Christian.

What more shall I say? For time would fail me to speak of Hale, learned in the law; of Addison, admired in the schools; of Milton, celebrated among the poets; and of Washington, immortal in the field and the cabinet. To this catalog of professing Christians, from among, if I may speak so, a higher order of beings, may now be added the name of Alexander Hamilton—a name which raises in the mind the idea of whatever is great, whatever is splendid, whatever is illustrious in human nature; and which is now added to a catalog which might be lengthened—and lengthened—and lengthened, with the names of illustrious characters whose lives have blessed society and whose works form a column high as heaven; a column of learning, of wisdom, and of greatness, which will stand to future ages, an eternal monument of the transcendent talents of the advocates of Christianity, when every fugitive leaf from the pen of the canting infidel witlings of the day shall be swept by the tide of time from the annals of the world and buried with the names of their authors in oblivion.

Everything else is fugitive; everything else is mutable; everything else will fail you. But this, the citadel of the Christian's hopes, will never fail you. Its base is adamant. It is cemented with the richest blood. The ransomed of the Lord crowd its portals. Embosomed in the dust which it encloses, the bodies of the redeemed "rest in hope." On its top dwells the Church of the first-born, who in delightful response with the angels of light chant redeeming love. Against this citadel the tempest beats, and around it the storm rages and spends its force in vain. Immortal in its nature, and incapable of change, it stands, and stands firm, amid the ruins of a moldering world, and endures for ever.

Thither fly, ye prisoners of hope!—that when earth, air, elements, shall have passed away, secure of existence and felicity, you may join with saints in glory to perpetuate the song which lingered on the faltering tongue of Hamilton, "Grace—rich Grace." God grant us this honor. Then shall the measure of our joy be full, and to His name shall be the glory in Christ.

JOHN RANDOLPH

ON OFFENSIVE WAR WITH ENGLAND [1]

(1806)

Born in 1773, died in 1833; Member of Congress in 1799-1813; in
1815-17, and in 1819-25; United States Senator in 1825-27; Member
of Congress in 1827-29; Minister to Russia in 1830: again elected to
Congress in 1832.

I AM perfectly aware that upon entering on
this subject we go into it manacled, handcuffed,
and tongue-tied. Gentlemen know that our lips
are sealed in subjects of momentous foreign relations which are indissolubly linked with the
present question, and which would serve to
throw a great light on it in every respect rele-
vant to it. I will, however, endeavor to hobble
over the subject as well as my fettered limbs
and palsied tongue will enable me to do it.

I am not surprised to hear this resolution
discussed by its friends as a war measure. They
say, it is true, that it is not a war measure; but
they defend it on principles which would justify
none but war measures, and seem pleased with
the idea that it may prove the forerunner of
war. If war is necessary, if we have reached
this point, let us have war. But while I have

<hr>

[1] Delivered in the House of Representatives on March 5, 1806.
Owing to differences with Great Britain it had been proposed that
British manufacturers be excluded from importation. Abridged.

life I will never consent to these incipient war measures which in their commencement breathe nothing but peace, tho they plunge us at last into war.

Do gentlemen remember the capture of Cornwallis on land because De Grasse maintained the dominion of the ocean? To my mind no position is more clear than that if we go to war with Great Britain, Charleston and Boston, the Chesapeake and the Hudson, will be invested by British squadrons. Will you call on the Count de Grasse to relieve them? or shall we apply to Admiral Gravina, or Admiral Villeneuve, to raise the blockade?

What is the question in dispute? The carrying trade. What part of it? The fair, the honest, and the useful trade that is engaged in carrying our own production to foreign markets and bringing back their productions in exchange? No, sir; it is that carrying trade which covers enemy's property and carries the coffee, the sugar, and other West India products to the mother country.

No, sir; if this great agricultural nation is to be governed by Salem and Boston, New York and Philadelphia, and Baltimore and Norfolk and Charleston, let gentlemen come out and say so; and let a committee of public safety be appointed from those towns to carry on the government.

I, for one, will not mortgage my property and my liberty to carry on this trade. The nation said so seven years ago; I said so then, and I say so now. It is not for the honest carrying trade of America, but for this mushroom, this fungus of war—for a trade which, as soon as the nations of Europe are at peace, will no longer exist; it is for this that the spirit of avaricious traffic would plunge us into war.

But we are asked, are we willing to bend the neck to England; to submit to her outrages? No, sir; I answer that it will be time enough for us to tell gentlemen what we will do to vindicate the violation of our flag on the ocean when they shall have told us what they have done in resentment of the violation of the actual territory of the United States by Spain, the true territory of the United States—not your new-fangled country over the Mississippi, but the good old United States—part of Georgia, of the old thirteen States, where citizens have been taken, not from our ships, but from our actual territory. When gentlemen have taken the padlock from our mouths I shall be ready to tell them what I will do relative to our dispute with Britain on the law of nations, on contraband, and such stuff.

France is at war with England; suppose her power on the continent of Europe no greater than it is on the ocean. How would she make her enemy feel it? There would be a perfect non-conductor between them. So with the United States and England; she scarcely presents to us a vulnerable point. Her commerce is carried on, for the most part, in fleets; where in single ships, they are stout and well armed— very different from the state of her trade during the American War, when her merchantmen became the prey of paltry privateers. Great Britain has been too long at war with the three most powerful maritime nations of Europe not to have learnt how to protect her trade. She can afford convoy to it all; she has eight hundred ships in commission: the navies of her enemies are annihilated.

Thus this war has presented the new and curious political spectacle of a regular annual increase (and to an immense amount) of her imports and exports, and tonnage and revenue, and all the insignia of accumulating wealth, while in every former war, without exception, these have suffered a greater or less diminution. And wherefore? Because she has driven France, Spain, and Holland from the ocean. Their marine is no more. I verily believe that ten English ships of the line would not decline a meeting with the combined fleets of those nations.

But this is not my only objection to entering upon this naval warfare. I am averse to a naval war with any nation whatever. I was opposed to the naval war of the last administration, and I am as ready to oppose a naval war of the present administration should they meditate such a measure. What! shall this great mammoth of the American forest leave his native element and plunge into the water in a mad contest with the shark? Let him beware that his proboscis is not bitten off in the engagement. Let him stay on shore, and not be excited by the mussels and periwinkles on the strand, or political bears, in a boat to venture on the perils of the deep.

Gentlemen say, Will you not protect your violated rights? and I say, Why take to water, where you can neither fight nor swim? Look at France; see her vessels stealing from port to port on her own coast; and remember that she is the first military power of the earth, and as a naval people second only to England. Take away the British navy, and France to-morrow is the tyrant of the ocean.

This brings me to the second point. How far it is politic in the United States to throw their weight into the scale of France at this moment?—from whatever motive to aid the views of her gigantic ambition—to make her mistress of the sea and land—to jeopardize the liberties of mankind. Sir, you may help to crush Great Britain—you may assist in breaking down her naval dominion, but you can not succeed to it. The iron scepter of the ocean will pass into his hands who wears the iron crown of the land. You may then expect a new code of maritime law. Where will you look for redress?

But, sir, I have yet a more cogent reason against going to war for the honor of the flag in the narrow seas, or any other maritime punctilio. It springs from my attachment to the principles of the government under which I live. I declare, in the face of day, that this government was not instituted for the purposes of offensive war. No; it was framed, to use its own language, for the common defense and the general welfare, which are inconsistent with offensive war.

I call that offensive war which goes out of our jurisdiction and limits, for the attainment or protection of objects not within those limits and that jurisdiction. As in 1798 I was opposed to this species of warfare because I believer it would raze the Constitution to the very foundation, so in 1806 I am opposed to it, and on the same grounds. No sooner do you put the Constitution to this use—to a test which it is by no means calculated to endure, than its incompetency to such purposes becomes manifest and apparent to all. I fear, if you go into a foreign war for a circuitous, unfair carrying trade, you will come out without your Constitution. Have you not contractors enough in this House? Or do you want to be overrun and devoured by commissaries and all the vermin of contract?

For my part I never will go to war but in self-defense. I have no desire for conquests— no ambition to possess Nova Scotia; I hold the liberties of this people at a higher rate. Much more am I indisposed to war when among the first means for carrying it on I see gentlemen propose the confiscation of debts due by government to individuals. Does a *bona fide* creditor know who holds his paper? Dare any honest man ask himself the question? 'Tis hard to say whether such principles are more detestably dishonest than they are weak and foolish. What, sir; will you go about with proposals for opening a loan in one hand and a sponge for the national debt in the other?

But the gentleman has told you that we ought to go to war, if for nothing else, for the fur trade. Now, sir, the people on whose support he seems to calculate, follow, let me tell him, a better business; and let me add that while men are happy at home reaping their own fields, the fruits of their labor and industry, there is little danger of their being induced to go sixteen or seventeen hundred miles in pursuit of beavers, raccoons or opossums—much less of going to war for the privilege. They are better employed where they are.

This trade, sir, may be important to Britain, to nations who have exhausted every resource of industry at home—bowed down by taxation and wretchedness. Let them, in God's name, if they please, follow the fur trade. They may, for me, catch every beaver in North America. Yes, sir, our people have a better occupation—a safe, profitable, honorable employment.

Gentlemen may take notes if they please; but I will never, from any motives short of self-defense, enter upon war. I will never be instrumental to the ambitious schemes of Bonaparte, nor put into his hands what will enable him to wield the world; and on the very principle that I wished success to the French arms in 1793. And wherefore? Because the case is changed. Great Britain can never again see the year 1760. Her Continental influence is gone for ever. Let who will be uppermost on the continent of Europe, she must find more than a counterpoise for her strength. Her race is run. She can only be formidable as a maritime power; and even as such perhaps not long. Are you going to justify the acts of the last administration, for which they have been deprived of the government, at our instance? Are you going back to the ground of 1798-9?

But, sir, as French is the fashion of the day, I may be asked for my *projet*. I can readily tell gentlemen what I will not do. I will not propitiate any foreign nation with money. I will not launch into a naval war with Great Britain, altho I am ready to meet her at the Cowpens or Bunker's Hill. And for this plain reason.

We are a great land animal, and our business is on shore. I will send her no money, sir, on any pretext whatsoever, much less on pretense of buying Labrador or Botany Bay, when my real object was to secure limits which she formally acknowledged at the peace of 1783. I go further—I would (if anything) have laid an embargo. This would have got our own property home and our adversary's into our power. If there is any wisdom left among us the first step toward hostility will always be an embargo. In six months all your mercantile megrims would vanish. As to us, altho it would cut deep, we can stand it. Without such a precaution, go to war when you will, you go to the wall. As to debts, strike the balance to-morrow and England is, I believe, in our debt.

I hope, sir, to be excused for proceeding in this desultory course. I flatter myself I shall not have occasion again to trouble you; I know not that I shall be able—certainly not willing, unless provoked in self-defense. I ask your attention to the character of the inhabitants of that southern country on whom gentlemen rely for the support of their measure. Who and what are they? A simple agricultural people, accustomed to travel in peace to market with the produce of their labor. Who takes it from us?

Another people devoted to manufactures— our sole source of supply. I have seen some stuff in the newspapers about manufacturers in Saxony, and about a man who is no longer the chief of a dominant faction. The greatest man whom I ever knew—the immortal author of the letters of Curtius [1]—has remarked the prone-

---

[1] Several writers had then been using the signature "Curtius"— Noah Webster in 1795 in sustaining the Jay treaty with England; John Thompson (Richmond) 1804, and another writer whom Cush-

ness of cunning people to wrap up and disguise, in well-selected phrases, doctrines too deformed and detestable to bear exposure in naked words; by a judicious choice of epithets to draw the attention from the lurking principle beneath and perpetuate delusion. But a little while ago, and any man might be proud to be considered as the head of the Republican party. Now, it seems, 'tis reproachful to be deemed the chief of a dominant faction.

Mr. Chairman, I am sensible of having detained the committee longer than I ought—certainly much longer than I intended. I am equally sensible of their politeness, and not less so, sir, of your patient attention. It is your own indulgence, sir, badly requited indeed, to which you owe this persecution. I might offer another apology for these undigested, desultory remarks—my never having seen the treasury documents. Until I came into the House this morning I have been stretched on a sick bed.

ing ("Initials and Pseudonyms") believes was John Taylor. Taylor's papers were published as "A Defense of the Measures of the Administration of Thomas Jefferson" (Washington, 1804).

EVERETT

THE ISSUE IN THE REVOLUTION [1]

(1825)

Born in 1794, died in 1865; made Professor of Greek at Harvard in 1819; elected to Congress in 1825; Governor of Massachusetts in 1836; Minister to England in 1841; President of Harvard in 1846; Secretary of State in 1852; Senator from Massachusetts in 1853.

IT belongs to us with strong propriety to celebrate this day. The town of Cambridge and the county of Middlesex are filled with the vestiges of the Revolution; whithersoever we turn our eyes we behold some memento of its glorious scenes. Within the walls in which we are now assembled was convened the first provincial Congress after its adjournment at Concord. The rural magazine at Medford reminds us of one of the earliest acts of British aggression.

The march of both divisions of the royal army on the memorable 19th of April was through the limits of Cambridge; in the neighboring towns of Lexington and Concord the first blood of the Revolution [2] was shed; in West

[1] From an address in Cambridge on the fiftieth anniversary of American Independence.

[2] The Battle of Golden Hill, fought in John Street, New York City, in September, 1770, being in a sense a part of the War of the Revolution, since it was fought between British soldiers and the Sons of Liberty, it has been held that the first blood of the Revolution was shed there instead of at Lexington.

196

Cambridge the royal convoy of provisions was, the same day, gallantly surprised by the aged citizens who stayed to protect their homes while their sons pursued the foe.

Here the first American army was formed; from this place, on the 17th of June, was detached the Spartan band that immortalized the heights of Charlestown and consecrated that day with blood and fire to the cause of American liberty. Beneath the venerable elm which still shades the southwestern corner of the common, General Washington first unsheathed his sword at the head of an American army, and to that seat was wont every Sunday to repair to join in the supplications which were made for the welfare of his country.

How changed is now the scene! The foe is gone! The din and the desolation of war are passed; science has long resumed her station in the shades of our venerable university, no longer glittering with arms; the anxious war council is no longer in session, to offer a reward for the discovery of the best mode of making saltpeter—an unpromising stage of hostilities when an army of twenty thousand men is in the field in front of the foe; the tall grass now waves in the trampled sallyport of some of the rural redoubts that form a part of the simple lines of circumvallation within which a half-armed American militia held the flower of the British army blockaded; the plow has done what the English batteries could not do—has leveled others of them with the earth; and the men, the great and good men, their warfare is over and they have gone quietly down to the dust they redeemed from oppression.

At the close of a half century since the declaration of our independence we are assembled to commemorate that great and happy event. We come together, not because it needs, but because it deserves these acts of celebration. We do not meet each other and exchange our felicitations because we should otherwise fall into forgetfulness of this auspicious era, but because we owe it to our fathers and to our children to mark its return with grateful festivities.

The major part of this assembly is composed of those who had not yet engaged in the active scenes of life when the Revolution commenced. We come not to applaud our own work but to pay a filial tribute to the deeds of our fathers. It was for their children that the heroes and sages of the Revolution labored and bled. They were too wise not to know that it was not personally their own cause in which they were embarked; they felt that they were engaging in an enterprise which an entire generation must be too short to bring to its mature and perfect issue.

The most they could promise themselves was, that, having cast forth the seed of liberty, having shielded its tender germ from the stern blasts that beat upon it, having watered it with the tears of waiting eyes and the blood of brave hearts, their children might gather the fruit of its branches, while those who planted it should molder in peace beneath its shade.

Nor was it only in this that we discern their disinterestedness, their heroic forgetfulness of self. Not only was the independence for which they struggled a great and arduous adventure, of which they were to encounter the risk and others to enjoy the benefits, but the oppressions which roused them had assumed in their day no worse form than that of a pernicious principle. No tolerable acts of oppression had ground them to the dust. They were not slaves rising in desperation from beneath the agonies of the lash, but free men, snuffing from afar "the tainted gale of tyranny."

The worse encroachments on which the British ministry had ventured might have been borne consistently with the practical enjoyment of many of the advantages resulting from good government. On the score of calculation alone that generation had much better have paid the duties on glass, painter's colors, stamped paper, and tea, than have plunged into the expenses of the Revolutionary War.

But they thought not of shuffling off upon posterity the burden of resistance. They well understood the part which providence had assigned to them. They perceived that they were called to discharge a high and perilous office to the cause of freedom; that their hands were elected to strike the blow for which nearly two centuries of preparation—never remitted, tho often unconscious—had been making on one side or the other of the Atlantic. They felt that the Colonies had now reached that stage in their growth when the difficult problem of colonial government must be solved—difficult I call it, for such it is to the statesman whose mind is not sufficiently enlarged for the idea that a wise colonial government must naturally and rightfully end in independence; that even a mild and prudent sway on the part of the mother country furnishes no reason for not severing the bands of the colonial subjection; and that when the rising State has passed the period of adolescence the only alternative which remains is that of a peaceable separation or a convulsive rupture.

The British ministry, at that time weaker than it had ever been since the infatuated reign of James II., had no knowledge of political science but that which they derived from the text of official records. They drew their maxims, as it was happily said of one of them that he did his measures, from the file. They heard that a distant province had resisted the execution of an act of Parliament. Indeed, and what is the specific in cases of resistance?—a military force; and two more regiments are ordered to Boston. Again they hear that the general court of Massachusetts Bay has taken counsels subversive of the allegiance due to the

Crown. A case of a refractory corporation; what is to be done? First try a mandamus, and if that fails seize the franchises into his majesty's hands.

They never asked the great questions: whether nations, like men, have not their principles of growth; whether providence has assigned no laws to regulate the changes in the condition of that most astonishing of human things, a nation of kindred men. They did not inquire, I will not say whether it were rightful and expedient, but whether it were practicable, to give law across the Atlantic to a people who possessed within themselves every imaginable element of self-government—a people rocked in the cradle of liberty, brought up to hardship, inheriting nothing but their rights on earth and their hopes in heaven.

But tho the rulers of Britain appear not to have caught a glimpse of the great principles involved in these questions, our fathers had asked and answered them. They perceived with the rapidity of intuition that the hour of separation had come; because a principle was assumed by the British government which put an instantaneous check to the further growth of liberty. Either the race of civilized man happily planted on our shores, at first slowly and painfully reared, but at length auspiciously multiplying in America, is destined never to constitute a free and independent State, or these measures must be resisted which go to bind it in a mild but abject colonial vassalage.

A mighty question of political right was at issue between the two hemispheres. Europe and America in the face of mankind are going to plead the great cause on which the fate of popular government for ever is suspended. One circumstance, and one alone, exists to diminish the interest of the contention—the perilous inequality of the parties—an inequality far exceeding that which gives animation to a contest, and so great as to destroy the hope of an ably waged encounter.

On the one side were arrayed the two houses of the British Parliament, the modern school of political eloquence, the arena where great minds had for a century and a half strenuously wrestled themselves into strength and power, and in better days the common and upright chancery of an empire on which the sun never set.

Upon the other side rose up the colonial assemblies of Massachusetts and Virginia, and the Continental Congress of Philadelphia, composed of men whose training had been within a small provincial circuit; who had never before felt the inspiration which the consciousness of a station before the world imparts; who brought no power into the contest but that which they drew from their cause and their bosoms.

It is by champions like these that the great principles of representative government, of chartered rights and constitutional liberty are to be discussed; and surely never in the annals of national controversy was exhibited a triumph so complete of the seemingly weaker party, a rout so disastrous of the stronger. Often as it has been repeated, it will bear another repetition; it never ought to be omitted in the history of constitutional liberty; it ought especially to be repeated this day; the various addresses, petitions, and appeals, the correspondence, the resolutions, the legislative and popular debates, from 1764 to the Declaration of Independence, present a maturity of political wisdom, a strength of argument, a gravity of style, a manly eloquence, and a moral courage, of which unquestionably the modern world affords no other example.

This need of praise, substantially accorded at the time by Chatham, in the British Parliament, may well be repeated by us. For most of the venerated men to whom it is paid it is but a pious tribute to departed worth. The Lees and the Henrys, Otis, Quincy, Warren, and Samuel Adams, the men who spoke those words of thrilling power which raised and ruled the storm of resistance and rang like the voice of fate across the Atlantic, are beyond the reach of our praise.

JACKSON

I

HIS SECOND INAUGURAL ADDRESS [1]
(1833)

Born in 1767, died in 1845; elected to Congress in 1796, and to the United States Senate in 1797; defeated the Creek Indians in 1813–14; won the Battle of New Orleans in 1815; fought the Seminole Indians in 1817–18; Governor of Florida in 1821; United States Senator in 1823; defeated for the Presidency in 1824; elected President in 1828; reelected in 1832; vetoed the Bill rechartering the Bank of the United States in 1832; suppressed nullification in South Carolina in 1832.

THE will of the American people, expressed through their unsolicited suffrages, calls me before you to pass through the solemnities preparatory to taking upon myself the duties of president of the United States for another term. For their approbation of my public conduct through a period which has not been without its difficulties, and for this renewed expression of their confidence in my good intentions, I am at a loss for terms adequate to the expression of my gratitude.

It shall be displayed to the extent of my humble abilities in continued efforts so to administer the government as to preserve their liberty and promote their happiness.

[1] Delivered on March 4, 1833.

204

So many events have occurred within the last four years which have necessarily called forth—sometimes under circumstances the most delicate and painful—my views of the principles and policy which ought to be pursued by the general government, that I need on this occasion but allude to a few leading considerations connected with some of them.

The foreign policy adopted by our government soon after the formation of our present Constitution, and very generally pursued by successive administrations, has been crowned with almost complete success, and has elevated our character among the nations of the earth. To do justice to all and to submit to wrong from none has been during my administration its growing maxim, and so happy have been its results that we are not only at peace with all the world, but have few causes of controversy, and those of minor importance, remaining unadjusted.

In the domestic policy of this government, there are two objects which especially deserve the attention of the people and their representatives, and which have been and will continue to be the subjects of my increasing solicitude. They are the preservation of the rights of the several States and the integrity of the Union.

These great objects are necessarily connected, and can only be attained by an enlightened exercise of the powers of each within its appropriate sphere, in conformity with the public will constitutionally expressed. To this end it becomes the duty of all to yield a ready and patriotic submission to the laws constitutionally enacted, and thereby promote and strengthen a proper confidence in those institutions of the several States and of the United States which the people themselves have ordained for their own government.

My experience in public concerns and the observation of a life somewhat advanced confirm the opinions long since imbibed by me, that the destruction of our State governments or the annihilation of their control over the local concerns of the people would lead directly to revolution and anarchy, and finally to despotism and military domination. In proportion, therefore, as the general government encroaches upon the rights of the States, in the same proportion does it impair its own power and detract from its ability to fulfil the purposes of its creation. Solemnly impressed with these considerations, my countrymen will ever find me ready to exercise my constitutional powers in arresting measures which may directly or indirectly encroach upon the rights of the States or tend to consolidate all political power in the general government. But of equal, and, indeed, of incalculable importance is the union of these States, and the sacred duty of all to contribute to its preservation by a liberal support of the general government in the exercise of its just powers. You have been wisely admonished to "accustom yourselves to think and speak of the Union as the palladium of your political safety and prosperity, watching for its preservation with jealous anxiety, discountenancing whatever may suggest even a suspicion that it can, in any event, be abandoned, and indignantly frowning upon the first dawning of any attempt to alienate any portion of our country from the rest, or to enfeeble the sacred ties which now link together the various parts." Without union our independence and liberty would never have been achieved; without union they never can be maintained. Divided into twenty-four, or even a smaller number, of separate communities, we shall see our internal trade burdened with numberless restraints and exactions; communication between distant points and sections obstructed or cut off; our sons made soldiers to deluge with blood the fields they now till in peace; the mass of our people borne down and impoverished by taxes to support armies and navies, and military leaders at the head of their victorious legions becoming our lawgivers and judges. The loss of liberty, of all good government, of peace, plenty, and happiness, must inevitably follow a dissolution of the Union. In supporting it, therefore, we support all that is dear to the freeman and the philanthropist.

The time at which I stand before you is full of interest. The eyes of all nations are fixed on our Republic. The event of the existing crisis will be decisive in the opinion of mankind of the practicability of our federal system of government. Great is the stake placed in our hands; great is the responsibility which must rest upon the people of the United States. Let us realize the importance of the attitude in which we stand before the world. Let us exercise forbearance and firmness. Let us extricate our country from the dangers which surround it, and learn wisdom from the lessons they inculate.

Deeply impressed with the truth of these observations, and under the obligation of that solemn oath which I am about to take, I shall continue to exert all my faculties to maintain the just powers of the Constitution and to transmit unimpaired to posterity the blessings of our federal Union. At the same time it will be my aim to inculcate by my official acts the necessity of exercising by the general government those powers only that are clearly delegated; to encourage simplicity and economy in the expenditures of the government; to raise no more money from the people than may be requisite for these objects, and in a manner that will best promote the interests of all classes of the community and of all portions of the Union. Constantly bearing in mind that in entering into society "individuals must give up a share of liberty to preserve the rest," it will be my desire so to discharge my duties as to foster with our brethren in all parts of the country a spirit of liberal concession and compromise, and, by reconciling our fellow citizens to those partial sacrifices which they must unavoidably make for the preservation of a greater good, to recommend our invaluable government and Union to the confidence and affections of the American people.

Finally, it is my most fervent prayer to that Almighty Being before whom I now stand, and who has kept us in His hands from the infancy of our Republic to the present day, that He will so overrule all my intentions and actions and inspire the hearts of my fellow citizens that we may be preserved from dangers of all kinds and continue for ever a united and happy people.

II

HIS FAREWELL ADDRESS [1]

(1837)

THE necessity of watching with jealous anxiety for the preservation of the Union was earnestly pressed upon his fellow citizens by the Father of his Country in his farewell address. He has there told us that "while experience shall not have demonstrated its impracticability, there will always be reason to distrust the patriotism of those who, in any quarter, may endeavor

---

[1] On retiring from the presidency in 1837. Jackson spent the remainder of his life at The Hermitage, his home, near Nashville, Tennessee, where he died in 1845. Abridged.

to weaken its bonds''; and he has cautioned us in the strongest terms against the formation of parties on geographical discriminations as one of the means which might disturb our Union, and to which designing men would be likely to resort.

The lessons contained in this invaluable legacy of Washington to his countrymen should be cherished in the heart of every citizen to the latest generation; and perhaps at no period of time could they be more usefully remembered than at the present moment. For when we look upon the scenes that are passing around us, and dwell upon the pages of his parting address, his paternal counsels would seem to be not merely the offspring of wisdom and foresight, but the voice of prophecy foretelling events and warning us of the evil to come. Forty years have passed since that imperishable document was given to his countrymen. The federal Constitution was then regarded by him as an experiment, and he so speaks of it in his address; but an experiment upon the success of which the best hopes of his country depended, and we all know that he was prepared to lay down his life, if necessary, to secure to it a full and fair trial. The trial has been made. It has succeeded beyond the proudest hopes of those who framed it. Every quarter of this widely extended nation has felt its blessings and shared in the general prosperity produced by its adoption.

But amid this general prosperity and splendid success, the dangers of which he warned us are becoming every day more evident, and the signs of evil are sufficiently apparent to awaken the deepest anxiety in the bosom of the patriot. We behold systematic efforts publicly made to sow the seeds of discord between different parts of the United States, and to place party divisions directly upon geographical distinctions; to excite the South against the North, and the North against the South, and to force into the controversy the most delicate and exciting topics upon which it is impossible that a large portion of the Union can ever speak without strong emotions. Appeals, too, are constantly made to sectional interests, in order to influence the election of the chief magistrate, as if it were desired that he should favor a particular quarter of the country instead of fulfilling the duties of his station with impartial justice to all; and the possible dissolution of the Union has at length become an ordinary and familiar subject of discussion.

Has the warning voice of Washington been forgotten? or have designs already been formed to sever the Union? Let it not be supposed that I impute to all of those who have taken an active part in these unwise and unprofitable discussions a want of patriotism or of public virtue. The honorable feeling of State pride and local attachments find a place in the bosoms of the most enlightened and pure. But while such men are conscious of their own integrity and honesty of purpose they ought never to forget that the citizens of other States are their political brethren; and that, however mistaken they may be in their views, the great body of them are equally honest and upright with themselves. Mutual suspicions and reproaches may in time create mutual hostility, and artful and designing men will always be found who are ready to foment these fatal divisions and to inflame the natural jealousies of different sections of the country. The history of the world is full of such examples, and especially the history of republics.

What have you to gain by division and dissension? Delude not yourselves with the belief that a breach once made may be afterward repaired. If the Union is once severed, the line of separation will grow wider and wider, and the controversies which are now debated and settled in the halls of legislation will then be tried in fields of battle and be determined by the sword. Neither should you deceive yourselves with the hope that the first line of separation would be the permanent one, and that nothing but harmony and concord would be found in the new associations formed upon the dissolution of this Union. Local interests would still be found there, and unchastened ambition. And if the recollection of common dangers, in which the people of these United States stood side by side against the common foe; the memory of victories won by their united valor; the prosperity and happiness they have enjoyed under the present Constitution; the proud name they bear as citizens of this great Republic,—if these recollections and proofs of common interest are not strong enough to bind us together as one people, what tie will hold this Union dissevered?

The first line of separation would not last for a single generation; new fragments would be torn off; new leaders would spring up; and this great and glorious Republic would soon be broken into a multitude of petty States armed for mutual aggressions, loaded with taxes to pay armies and leaders, seeking aid against each other from foreign powers, insulted and trampled upon by the nations of Europe, until, harassed with conflicts, and humbled and debased in spirit, they would be ready to submit to the absolute dominion of any military adventurer, and to surrender their liberty for the sake of repose. It is impossible to look on the consequences that would inevitably follow the destruction of this government, and not feel indignant when we hear cold calculations about the value of the Union and have so constantly before us a line of conduct so well calculated to weaken its ties.

There is too much at stake to allow pride or passion to influence your decision. Never for a moment believe that the great body of the citizens of any State or States can deliberately intend to do wrong. They may, under the influence of temporary excitement or misguided opinions, commit mistakes; they may be misled for a time by the suggestions of self-interest; but in a community so enlightened and patriotic as the people of the United States, argument will soon make them sensible of their errors, and, when convinced, they will be ready to repair them. If they have no higher or better motives to govern them, they will at least perceive that their own interest requires them to be just to others as they hope to receive justice at their hands.

But in order to maintain the Union unimpaired, it is absolutely necessary that the laws passed by the constituted authorities should be faithfully executed in every part of the country, and that every good citizen should at all times stand ready to put down, with the combined force of the nation, every attempt at unlawful resistance, under whatever pretext it may be made or whatever shape it may assume. Unconstitutional or oppressive laws may no doubt be passed by Congress, either from erroneous views or the want of due consideration; if they are within reach of judicial authority, the remedy is easy and peaceful, and if, from the character of the law, it is an abuse of power not within the control of the judiciary, then free discussion and calm appeals to reason and to the justice of the people will not fail to redress the wrong. But until the law shall be declared void by the courts or repealed by Congress, no individual or combination of individuals can be justified in forcibly resisting its execution. It is impossible that any government can continue to exist upon any other principles. It would cease to be a government, and be unworthy of the name, if it had not the power to enforce the execution for its own laws within its own sphere of action.

It is true that cases may be imagined disclosing such a settled purpose of usurpation and oppression on the part of the government as would justify an appeal to arms. These, however, are extreme cases, which we have no reason to apprehend in a government where the power is in the hands of a patriotic people; and no citizen who loves his country would in any case whatever resort to forcible resistance unless he clearly saw that the time had come when a freeman should prefer death to submission; for if such a struggle is once begun, and the citizens of one section of the country be arrayed in arms against those of another in doubtful conflict, let the battle result as it may, there will be an end of the Union, and with it an end of the hopes of freedom. The victory of the injured would not secure to them the blessings of liberty; it would avenge their wrongs, but they would themselves share in the common ruin.

But the Constitution can not be maintained, nor the Union preserved, in opposition to pub-

lic feeling, by the mere exertion of the coercive
powers confided to the general government. The
foundations must be laid in the affections of
the people; in the security it gives to life, liberty, character, and property, in every quarter
of the country; and in the fraternal attachments which the citizens of the several States
bear to one another, as members of one political family mutually contributing to promote
the happiness of each other. Hence the citizens
of every State should studiously avoid everything calculated to wound the sensibility or
offend the just pride of the people of other
States; and they should frown upon any proceedings within their own borders likely to disturb the tranquillity of their political brethren
in other portions of the Union.

You have no longer any cause to fear danger
from abroad; your strength and power are well
known throughout the civilized world, as well
as the high and gallant bearing of your sons. It
is from within, among yourselves, from cupid-
ity, from corruption, from disappointed ambition, and inordinate thirst for power, that
factions will be formed and liberty endangered.
It is against such designs, whatever disguise
the actors may assume, that you have especially to guard yourselves. You have the highest
of human trusts committed to your care. Providence has showered on this favored land blessings without number, and has chosen you, as
the guardians of freedom, to preserve it for the

benefit of the human race. May he who holds in his hands the destinies of nations make you worthy of the favors he has bestowed, and enable you, with pure hearts, and pure hands, and sleepless vigilance, to guard and defend to the end of time the great charge he has committed to your keeping.

My own race is nearly run; advanced age and failing health warn me that before long I must pass beyond the reach of human events and cease to feel the vicissitudes of human affairs. I thank God that my life has been spent in a land of liberty, and that he has given me a heart to love my country with the affection of a son. And filled with gratitude for your constant and unwavering kindness, I bid you a last and affectionate farewell.

SARGENT S. PRENTISS

ON THE DEATH OF LAFAYETTE[1]
(1835)

Born in 1808, died in 1850; elected to Congress from Mississippi in 1838.

DEATH who knocks with equal hand at the
door of the cottage and the palace gate, has
been busy at his appointed work. Mourning
prevails throughout the land, and the counte-
nances of all are shrouded in the mantle of regret. Far across the wild Atlantic, amid the
pleasant vineyards in the sunny land of France,
there, too, is mourning; and the weeds of sorrow are alike worn by prince and peasant.
Against whom has the monarch of the tomb
turned his remorseless dart that such wide-
spread sorrow prevails? Hark, and the agonized
voice of Freedom, weeping for her favorite son,
will tell you in strains sadder than those with
which she "shrieked when Kosciusko fell," that
Lafayette—the gallant and the good—has ceased
to live.

The friend and companion of Washington is
no more. He who taught the eagle of our
country, while yet unfledged, to plume his
young wing and mate his talons with the lion's

[1] From a speech at Jackson, Mississippi, in August, 1835.

strength, has taken his flight far beyond the stars, beneath whose influence he fought so well. Lafayette is dead! The gallant ship, whose pennon has so often bravely streamed above the roar of battle and the tempest's rage, has at length gone slowly down in the still and quiet waters. Well mightest thou, O Death, now recline beneath the laurels thou hast won; for never since, as the grim messenger of Almighty Vengeance, thou camest into this world, did a more generous heart cease to heave beneath thy chilling touch, and never will thy insatiate dart be hurled against a nobler breast! Who does not feel at the mournful intelligence, as if he had lost something cheering from his own path through life; as if some bright star, at which he had been accustomed frequently and fondly to gaze, had been suddenly extinguished in the firmament?

How came he here? Born to a high name and a rich inheritance, educated at a dissipated and voluptuous court, married to a young and beautiful woman,—how came he to break through the blandishments of love and the temptations of pleasure and thus be found fighting the battles of strangers, far away in the wilds of America? It was because, from his infancy, there had grown up in his bosom a passion more potent than all others: the love of liberty. Upon his heart a spark from the very altar of Freedom had fallen and he watched and cherished it with more than vestal

vigilance. This passionate love of liberty, this
fire which was thenceforth to glow unquenched
and undimmed, impelled him to break asunder
the ties both of pleasure and affection. He
heard that a gallant people had raised the
standard of revolt against oppression and he
hastened to join them. It was to him the cru-
sade of Liberty; and like a knight of the Holy
Cross, he had enlisted in the ranks of those who
had sworn to rescue her altars from the profane
touch of the tyrant.

More congenial to him by far were the hard-
ships, the dangers, and the freedom of the
American wilds than the ease, the luxury, and
the slavery of his native court. He exchanged
the voice of love for the savage yell and the
hostile shout; the gentle strains of the harp and
lute for the trumpet and drum, and the still
more terrible music of clashing arms. Nor did
he come alone or empty-handed. The people
in whose cause he was about to peril his life
and his fortune were too poor to afford him
even the means of conveyance, and his own
court threw every obstacle in the way of the
accomplishment of his wishes. Did this dampen
his ardor? Did this chill his generous aspira-
tion? No; it added new vigor to each.

Here we can not but pause to contemplate
two wonderful men, belonging to the same age
and to the same nation: Napoleon and Lafayette. Their names excite no kindred emotions;
their fates no kindred sympathies. Napoleon—

the child of Destiny—the thunderbolt of war—
the victor in a hundred battles—the dispenser
of thrones and dominions; he who scaled the
Alps and reclined beneath the Pyramids, whose
word was fate and whose wish was law. Lafayette—the volunteer of Freedom—the advocate of human rights—the defender of civil liberty—the patriot and the philanthropist—the
beloved of the good and the free. Napoleon—
the vanquished warrior, ignobly flying from the
field of Waterloo, the wild beast, ravaging all
Europe in his wrath, hunted down by the
banded and affrighted nations and caged far
away upon an ocean-girded rock. Lafayette—
a watchword by which men excite each other to
deeds of worth and noble daring; whose home
has become the mecca of freedom, toward which
the pilgrims of Liberty turn their eyes from
every quarter of the globe. Napoleon was the
red and fiery comet, shooting wildly through the
realms of space and scattering pestilence and
terror among the nations. Lafayette was the
pure and brilliant planet, beneath whose grateful beams the mariner directs his bark and the
shepherd tends his flocks. Napoleon died and a
few old warriors—the scattered relics of Ma-
rengo and of Austerlitz—bewailed their chief.
Lafayette is dead and the tears of a civilized
world attest how deep is the mourning for his
loss. Such is, and always will be, the difference of feeling toward a benefactor and a conqueror of the human race.

WENDELL PHILLIPS

ON THE MURDER OF LOVEJOY [1]

(1837)

Born in 1811, died in 1884; admitted to the Bar in 1834; the leading
Orator of the Abolitionists in 1837–61; President of the Antislavery Society in 1865–70; advocated woman suffrage and labor
reform; Labor and Prohibition Candidate for Governor of Massachusetts in 1870.

A COMPARISON has been drawn between the
events of the Revolution and the tragedy at
Alton. We have heard it asserted here in Faneuil Hall, that Great Britain had a right to tax
the Colonies; and we have heard the mob at
Alton, the drunken murderers of Lovejoy, compared to those patriot fathers who threw the tea

[1] Delivered in Faneuil Hall, Boston, on December 8, 1837, and
Phillips's first great success as a public orator. This meeting had
been called to denounce the murder of Lovejoy at Alton, Illinois,
while defending his printing-press, from which had been printed
antislavery literature. Speeches had been made at this Boston
meeting by Channing and others, when great astonishment was
evoked by a speech from the attorney-general of the commonwealth who in comparing the Alton attack on Lovejoy to the Boston
Tea Party, said Lovejoy had "died as the fool dieth." Phillips,
who followed this speaker, was then twenty-six years old. Only a
few months before he had first become identified with the Antislavery Society. George William Curtis has likened the speech to
Patrick Henry's "electrical warning to George III." He calls it
"the greatest of oratorical triumphs," and mentions Lincoln's
Gettysburg speech as the "third of three that are illustrious in
our history." Abridged.

overboard! Fellow citizens, is this Faneuil Hall doctrine? The mob at Alton were met to wrest from a citizen his just rights—met to resist the laws. We have been told that our fathers did the same; and the glorious mantle of Revolutionary precedent has been thrown over the mobs of our day. To make out their title to such defense the gentleman says that the British Parliament had a right to tax these Colonies.

It is manifest that, without this, his parallel falls to the ground; for Lovejoy had stationed himself within constitutional bulwarks. He was not only defending the freedom of the Press, but he was under his own roof, in arms with the sanction of the civil authority. The men who assailed him went against and over the laws. The mob, as the gentleman terms it—mob, forsooth! certainly we sons of the tea-spillers are a marvelously patient generation!—the "orderly mob" which assembled in the Old South to destroy the tea were met to resist, not the laws, but illegal exactions! Shame on the American who calls the tea tax and Stamp Act laws! Our fathers resisted, not the king's prerogative, but the king's usurpation. To find any other account, you must read our Revolutionary history upside down. Our State archives are loaded with arguments of John Adams to prove the taxes laid by the British Parliament unconstitutional—beyond its power. It was not till this was made out that the men of New England rushed to arms. The arguments of the

Council-chamber and the House of Representatives preceded and sanctioned the contest.

To draw the conduct of our ancestors into a precedent for mobs, for a right to resist laws we ourselves have enacted, is an insult to their memory. The difference between the excitements of those days and our own, which the gentleman in kindness to the latter has overlooked, is simply this: the men of that day went for the right, as secured by the laws. They were the people rising to sustain the laws and Constitution of the province. The rioters of our day go for their own wills, right or wrong. Sir, when I heard the gentleman lay down principles which place the murderers of Alton side by side with Otis and Hancock, with Quincy and Adams, I thought those pictured lips [pointing to the portraits in the Hall] would have broken into voice to rebuke the recreant American—the slanderer of the dead. The gentleman said that he should sink into insignificance if he dared not gainsay the principles of these resolutions. Sir, for the sentiments he has uttered, on soil consecrated by the prayers of Puritans and the blood of patriots, the earth should have yawned and swallowed him up.[1]

---

[1] The contemporary account of this scene says: "Applause and hisses were here heard, with cries of 'Take that back,' and then the uproar became so great that for a long time no one could be heard. 'Phillips or nobody,' cried one; 'Make him take back "recreant,"' cried another; and a third: 'He sha'n't go on till he takes it back.' Finally a man said: 'I did not come here to take

Fellow citizens, I can not take back my words. Surely, the attorney-general, so long and well known here, needs not the aid of your hisses against one so young as I am—my voice never before heard within these walls!

Another ground has been taken to excuse the mob, and throw doubt and discredit on the conduct of Lovejoy and his associates. Allusion has been made to what lawyers understand very well—the "conflict of laws." We are told that nothing but the Mississippi River rolls between St. Louis and Alton; and the conflict of laws somehow or other gives the citizens of the former a right to find fault with the defender of the Press for publishing his opinions so near their limits. Will the gentleman venture that argument before lawyers? How the laws of the two States could be said to come into conflict in such circumstances I question whether any lawyer in this audience can explain or understand. No matter whether the line that divides one sovereign State from another be an imaginary one or ocean-wide, the moment you cross it, the State you leave is blotted out of existence, so far as you are concerned. The Czar might as well claim to control the deliberations of Faneuil Hall, as the laws of Missouri demand rever-

any part in this discussion, nor do I intend to; but I do entreat you, fellow citizens, by everything you hold sacred—I conjure you by every association connected with this Hall, consecrated by our fathers to freedom of discussion—that you listen to every man who addresses you in a decorous manner.' Mr. Phillips then resumed."

ence, or the shadow of obedience, from an inhabitant of Illinois.

I must find some fault with the statement which has been made of the events at Alton. It has been asked why Lovejoy and his friends did not appeal to the executive—trust their defense to the police of the city. It has been hinted that, from hasty and ill-judged excitement, the men within the building provoked a quarrel, and that he fell in the course of it—one mob resisting another. Recollect, sir, that they did act with the approbation and sanction of the mayor. In strict truth there was no executive to appeal to for protection. The mayor acknowledged that he could not protect them. They asked him if it was lawful for them to defend themselves. He told them it was, and sanctioned their assembling in arms to do so. They were not, then, a mob; they were not merely citizens defending their own property; they were in some sense the *posse comitatus*, adopted for the occasion into the police of the city, acting under the order of a magistrate. It was civil authority resisting lawless violence. Where, then, was the imprudence? Is the doctrine to be sustained here that it is imprudent for men to aid magistrates in executing the laws?

Men are continually asking each other, had Lovejoy a right to resist? Sir, I protest against the question instead of answering it. Lovejoy did not resist, in the sense they mean. He did not throw himself back on the natural right of

self-defense. He did not cry anarchy, and let
slip the dogs of civil war, careless of the horrors
which would follow.

Sir, as I understand this affair, it was not an
individual protecting his property; it was not
one body of armed men resisting another, and
making the streets of a peaceful city run
blood with their contentions. It did not bring
back the scenes in old Italian cities, where family met family, and faction met faction, and
mutually trampled the laws under foot. No!
the men in that house were regularly enrolled
under the sanction of the mayor. There being
no militia in Alton, about seventy men were
enrolled with the approbation of the mayor.
These relieved each other every other night.
About thirty men were in arms on the night of
the sixth, when the press was landed. The next
evening it was not thought necessary to sum-
mon more than half that number: among these
was Lovejoy. It was, therefore, you perceive,
sir, the police of the city resisting rioters—civil
government breasting itself to the shock of lawless men.

Here is no question about the right of self-
defense. It is in fact simply this: Has the civil
magistrate a right to put down a riot?

It has been stated, perhaps inadvertently,
that Lovejoy or his comrades fired first. This
is denied by those who have the best means of
knowing. Guns were first fired by the mob.
After being twice fired on, those within the

building consulted together and deliberately returned the fire. But suppose they did fire first. They had a right so to do—not only the right which every citizen has to defend himself, but the further right which every civil officer has to resist violence. Even if Lovejoy fired the first gun, it would not lessen his claim to our sympathy or destroy his title to be considered a martyr in defense of a free Press. The question now is, did he act within the Constitution and the laws? The men who fell in State Street on the 5th of March, 1770, did more than Lovejoy is charged with. They were the first assailants. Upon some slight quarrel they pelted the troops with every missile within reach. Did this bate one jot of the eulogy with which Hancock and Warren hallowed their memory, hailing them as the first martyrs in the cause of American liberty?

If, sir, I had adopted what are called peace principles, I might lament the circumstances of this case. But all you who believe, as I do, in the right and duty of magistrates to execute the laws, join with me and brand as base hypocrisy the conduct of those who assemble year after year on the Fourth of July to fight over the battles of the Revolution, and yet "damn with faint praise" or load with obloquy the memory of this man who shed his blood in defense of life, liberty, property, and the freedom of the Press!

Imagine yourself present when the first news

of Bunker Hill Battle reached a New England town. The tale would have run thus: "The patriots are routed—the redcoats victorious—Warren lies dead upon the field." With what scorn would that Tory have been received who should have charged Warren with imprudence! who should have said that, bred a physician, he was "out of place" in that battle, and "died as the fool dieth!" How would the intimation have been received that Warren and his associates should have waited a better time? But, if success be indeed the only criterion of prudence, *Respice finem*—Wait till the end.

Mr. Chairman, from the bottom of my heart I thank that brave little band at Alton for resisting. We must remember that Lovejoy had fled from city to city; suffered the destruction of three presses patiently. At length he took counsel with friends; men of character, of tried integrity, of wide views, of Christian principle. They thought the crisis had come. It was full time to assert the laws. They saw around them, not a community like our own, of fixed habits, of character molded and settled, but one "in the gristle, not yet hardened into the bone of manhood." The people there, children of our older States, seem to have forgotten the blood-tried principles of their fathers the moment they lost sight of our New England hills. Something was to be done to show them the priceless value of the freedom of the Press, to bring back and set right their wandering and

confused ideas. He and his advisers looked out
on a community staggering like a drunken man,
indifferent to their rights, and confused in their
feelings. Deaf to argument, haply they might
be stunned into sobriety. They saw that of
which we can not judge: the necessity of resistance. Insulted law called for it. Public opinion, fast hastening on the downward course,
must be arrested.

Does not the event show they judged rightly?
Absorbed in a thousand trifles, how has the nation all at once come to a stand! Men begin, as
in 1776 and 1640, to discuss principles, to
weigh characters, to find out where they are.
Haply we may awake before we are borne over
the precipice.

I am glad, sir, to see this crowded house. It
is good for us to be here. When liberty is in
danger, Faneuil Hall has the right, it is her
duty, to strike the key-note for these United
States. I am glad, for one reason, that remarks such as those to which I have alluded
have been uttered here. The passage of these
resolutions, in spite of this opposition, led by
the attorney-general of the commonwealth, will
show more clearly, more decisively, the deep indignation with which Boston regards this outrage.

BANCROFT

THE PEOPLE IN ART, GOVERNMENT, AND RELIGION [1]

(1835)

Born in 1800, died in 1891; Collector of the Port of Boston in 1828–41; unsuccessful candidate for Governor of Massachusetts in 1844; Secretary of the Navy in 1845–46; United States Minister to Great Britain in 1846; Minister to Berlin in 1867.

THE material world does not change in its masses or in its powers. The stars shine with no more luster than when they first sang together in the glory of their birth. The flowers that gemmed the fields and the forests before America was discovered, now bloom around us in their season. The sun that shone on Homer shines on us in unchanging luster; the bow that beamed on the patriarch still glitters in the clouds. Nature is the same. For her no new forces are generated, no new capacities are discovered. The earth turns on its axis and perfects its revolutions, and renews its seasons without increase or advancement.

But a like passive destiny does not attach to the inhabitants of the earth. For them expectations of social improvement are no delusion; the hopes of philanthropy are more than a

---

[1] Delivered before the Adelphi Society of Williams College, in August, 1835. Abridged.

dream. The five senses do not constitute the whole inventory of our source of knowledge. They are the organs by which thought connects itself with the external universe; but the power of thought is not merged in the exercise of its instruments. We have functions which connect us with heaven, as well as organs which set us in relation with earth. We have not merely the senses to open to us the external world, but an internal sense, which places us in connection with the world of intelligence and the decrees of God. There is a spirit in man—not in the privileged few, not in those of us only who, by the favor of providence, have been nursed in public schools; it is in man: it is the attribute of the race. The spirit, which is the guide to truth, is the gracious gift to each member of the human family.

You can not discover a tribe of men, but you also find the charities of life, and the proofs of spiritual existence. Behold the ignorant Algonquin deposit a bow and quiver by the side of the departed warrior, and recognize his faith in immortality. See the Comanche chieftain, in the heart of our continent, inflict upon himself the severest penance, and reverence his confession of the needed atonement for sin. The barbarian who roams o'er the Western prairies has like passions and like endowments with ourselves. He bears with him the instinct of Deity, the consciousness of spiritual nature, the love of beauty, the rule of morality.

If reason is a universal faculty, universal decision is the nearest criterion of truth. The common mind winnows opinions; it is the sieve which separates error from certainty. The exercise by many of the same faculty on the same subject would naturally lead to the same conclusions. But if not, the very differences of opinion that arise prove the supreme judgment of the general mind. Truth is one. It never contradicts itself. One truth can not contradict another truth. Hence truth is the bond of union. But error not only contradicts truth but may contradict itself; so that there may be many errors and each at variance with the rest. Truth is therefore of necessity an element of harmony; error as necessarily an element of discord. Thus there can be no continuing universal judgment but a right one. Men can not agree in an absurdity; neither can they agree in a falsehood.

The little story of Paul and Virginia is a universal favorite. When it was first written the author read it aloud to a circle in Paris, composed of the wife of the prime minister and the choicest critics of France. They condemned it as dull and insipid. The author appealed to the public, and the children of all Europe reversed the decree of the Parisians. The judgment of children—that is, the judgment of the common mind under its most innocent and least imposing form—was more trustworthy than the criticism of the select refinement of the most polished city in the world.

Demosthenes of old formed himself to the perfection of eloquence by means of addresses to the crowd. The great comic poet of Greece, emphatically the poet of the vulgar mob, is distinguished above all others for the incomparable graces of his diction; and it is related of one of the most skilful writers in the Italian that when inquired of where he had learned the purity and nationality of his style, he replied, from listening to country people as they brought their produce to market.

In like manner the best government rests on the people and not on the few, on persons and not on property, on the free development of public opinion and not on authority; because the munificent Author of our being has conferred the gifts of mind upon every member of the human race without distinction of outward circumstances. Whatever of other possessions may be engrossed, the mind asserts its own independence. Lands, estates, the produce of mines, the prolific abundance of the seas, may be usurped by a privileged class. Avarice, assuming the form of ambitious power, may grasp realm after realm, subdue continents, compass the earth in its schemes of aggrandizement, and sigh after worlds, but mind eludes the power of appropriation; it exists only in its own individuality; it is a property which can not be confiscated and can not be torn away. It laughs at chance; it bursts from imprisonment; it defies monopoly. A government of equal rights must, therefore, rest upon mind, not wealth, not brute force; some of the moral intelligence of the community should rule the State. Prescription can no more assume to be a valid plea for political injustice; society studies to eradicate established abuses and to bring social institutions and laws into harmony with moral right; not dismayed by the natural and necessary imperfections of all human effort, and not giving way to despair because every hope does not at once ripen into fruit.

The public happiness is the true object of legislation and can be secured only by the masses of mankind, themselves awakened to a knowledge and care of their own interests. Our free institutions have reversed the false and ignoble distinctions between men, and, refusing to gratify the pride of caste, have acknowledged the common mind to be the true material for a commonwealth. Everything has hitherto been done for the happy few. It is not possible to endow an aristocracy with greater benefits than they have already enjoyed; there is no room to hope that individuals will be more highly gifted or more fully developed than the greatest sages of past times. The world can advance only through the culture of the moral and intellectual powers of the people. To accomplish this end by means of the people themselves is the highest purpose of government. If it be the duty of the individual to strive after a perfection like the perfection of God, how much more ought a nation to be the image of duty. The common mind is the true Parian marble fit to be wrought into the likeness to a God. The duty of America is to secure the culture and the happiness of the masses by their reliance on themselves.

It is not by vast armies, by immense natural resources, by accumulations of treasure, that the greatest results in modern civilization have been accomplished. The traces of the career of conquest pass away, hardly leaving a scar on the national intelligence. Famous battle-grounds of victory are most of them comparatively indifferent to the human race—barren fields of blood, the scourges of their times, but affecting the social condition as little as the raging of a pestilence. Not one benevolent institution, not one ameliorating principle in the Roman State was a voluntary concession of the aristocracy; each useful element was borrowed from the democracies of Greece or was a reluctant concession to the demands of the people. The same is true in modern political life. It is the confession of an enemy to democracy that "all the great and noble institutions of the world have come from popular efforts."

It is the uniform tendency of the popular element to elevate and bless humanity. The exact measure of the progress of civilization is the degree in which the intelligence of the common mind has prevailed over wealth and brute force; in other words, the measure of the progress of civilization is the progress of the people. Every great object connected with the benevolent exertions of the day has reference to the culture of those powers which are alone the common inheritance. For this the envoys of a religion cross seas and visit remotest isles; for this the Press in its freedom teems with the productions of maturest thought; for this philanthropists plan new schemes of education; for this halls in every city and village are open to the public instructor.

It is alone by infusing great principles into the common mind that revolutions in human society are brought about. They never have been, they never can be effected by superior individual excellence. The age of the Antonines is the age of the greatest glory of the Roman Empire. Men distinguished by every accomplishment of culture and science for a century in succession possessed undisputed sway over more than one hundred millions of men, until, at last, in the person of Marcus Aurelius, philosophy herself seemed to mount the throne. And did she stay the downward tendencies of the Roman Empire? Did she infuse new elements of life into the decaying constitution? Did she commence one great beneficent reform? Not one permanent amelioration was effected. Philosophy was clothed with absolute power; and yet absolute power accomplished nothing for humanity. It could accomplish nothing. Had it been possible, Aurelius would have wrought a change. Society can be regenerated, the human race can be advanced, only by moral principles diffused through the multitude.

And now let us take an opposite instance; let us see if amelioration follows when, in despite of tyranny, truth finds access to the common people. Christianity itself shall furnish me the example.

So completely was this greatest of all reforms carried forward in the vale of life, that the great moral revolution, the great step of God's providence in the education of the human race, was not observed by the Roman historians. Once, indeed, at this early period, the Christians are mentioned; for, in the reign of Nero, their purity being hateful to the corrupt, Nero abandoned them to persecution. In the darkness of midnight they were covered with pitch and set on fire to light the streets of Rome, and this singularity has been recorded. But their system of morals and religion, tho it was the new birth of the world, escaped all notice.

Paul, who was a Roman citizen, was beheaded just outside the walls of the eternal city; and Peter, who was a plebeian and could not claim the distinction of the ax and block, was executed on the cross, with his head downward to increase the pain of the indignity. Do you think the Roman emperor took notice of the names of these men when he signed their death-warrants? And yet, as they poured truth into the common mind, what series of kings, what lines of emperors, can compare with them in their influence on the destinies of mankind.

The irresistible tendency of the human race is therefore to advancement, for absolute power has never succeeded and can never succeed in suppressing a single truth. An idea once revealed may find its admission into every living breast and live there. Like God, it becomes immortal and omnipresent. The movement of the species is upward, irresistibly upward. The individual is often lost; providence never disowns the race. No principle once promulgated has ever been forgotten. No "timely tramp" of a despot's foot ever trod out one idea. The world can not retrograde; the dark ages can not return. Dynasties perish, seeds are buried, nations have been victims to error, martyrs for right; humanity has always been on the advance, gaining maturity, universality, and power.

No truth can perish, no truth can pass away; the flame is undying, tho generations disappear. Wherever moral truth has struck into being, humanity claims and guards the greatest bequest. Each generation gathers together imperishable children of the past, and increases them by new sons of light alike radiant with immortality.

BENTON

ON THE EXPUNGING RESOLUTION[1]

(1837)

Born in 1782, died in 1858; United States Senator from Missouri,
1821-51; Representative in Congress, 1853-55; Author of "Thirty
Years' View."

IT is now three years since the resolve was
adopted by the Senate which it is my present
motion to expunge from the journal; at the
moment that this resolve was adopted I gave notice of my intention to move to expunge it, and
then expressed my confident belief that the motion would eventually prevail. That expression
of confidence was not an ebullition of vanity or
a presumptuous calculation intended to accelerate the event it affected to foretell. It was
not a vain boast, or an idle assumption, but was
the result of a deep conviction of the injustice
done President Jackson, and a thorough reliance
upon the justice of the American people. I felt
that the president had been wronged; and my
heart told me that this wrong would be re-

---

[1] Delivered in the United States Senate January 12, 1837. Abridged
Benton's Expunging Resolution provided that from the Journal of
the Senate the censure passed on Jackson by the Senate in March,
1834, be erased. This censure related to Jackson's action with the
United States Bank. Benton's motion was carried four days after
he made this speech.

dressed. The event proves that I was not mistaken. The question of expunging this resolution has been carried to the people, and their decision has been had upon it.

Assuming that we have ascertained the will of the people on this great question, the inquiry presents itself how far the expression of that will ought to be conclusive of our action here. I hold that it ought to be binding and obligatory upon us; and that, not only upon the principles of representative government, which require obedience to the known will of the people, but also in conformity to the principles upon which the proceeding against President Jackson was conducted when the sentence against him was adopted. Then everything was done with especial reference to the will of the people. Their impulsion was assumed to be the sole motive to action; and to them the ultimate verdict was expressly referred. The whole machinery of alarm and pressure—every engine of political and moneyed power—was put in motion and worked for many months to excite the people against the president, and to stir up meetings, memorials, petitions, traveling committees, and distress deputations against him; and each symptom of popular discontent was hailed as an evidence of public will, and quoted here as proof that the people demanded the condemnation of the president. Not only legislative assemblies, and memorials from large assemblies were then produced here as evidence of public opinion, but the petitions of boys under age, the remonstrances of a few signers, and the results of the most inconsiderable elections were ostentatiously paraded and magnified as the evidence of the sovereign will of our constituents.

Thus, sir, the public voice was everything, while that voice, partially obtained through political and pecuniary machinations, was adverse to the president. Then the popular will was the shrine at which all worshiped. Now, when that will is regularly, soberly, repeatedly, and almost universally expressed through the ballotboxes at the various elections and turns out to be in favor of the president, certainly no one can disregard it, nor otherwise look at it than as the solemn verdict of the competent and ultimate tribunal upon an issue fairly made up, fully argued, and duly submitted for decision. As such verdict, I receive it. As the deliberate verdict of the sovereign people, I bow to it. I am content. I do not mean to reopen the case or to recommence the argument. I leave that work to others, if any others choose to perform it. For myself, I am content; and dispensing with further argument I shall call for judgment and ask to have execution done upon that unhappy journal which the verdict of millions of freemen finds guilty of bearing on its face an untrue, illegal, and unconstitutional sentence of condemnation against the approved president of the Republic.

But, while declining to reopen the argument
of this question, and refusing to tread over
again the ground already traversed, there is another and a different task to perform; one
which the approaching termination of President
Jackson's administration makes peculiarly proper at this time, and which it is my privilege and
perhaps my duty to execute, as being the suitable conclusion to the arduous contest in which
we have been so long engaged. I allude to the
general tenor of his administration and to its
effect, for good or for evil, upon the condition
of his country. This is the proper time for
such a view to be taken. The political existence
of this great man now draws to a close. In
little more than forty days he ceases to be an
object of political hope to any, and should cease
to be an object of political hate, or envy, to all.
Whatever of motive the servile and time-serv-
ing might have found in his exalted station for
raising the altar of adulation and burning the
incense of praise before him, that motive can
no longer exist. The dispenser of the patronage of an empire, the chief of this great confederacy of States, is soon to be a private individual, stripped of all power to reward or to
punish. His own thoughts, as he has shown us
in the concluding paragraph of that message
which is to be the last of its kind that we shall
ever receive from him, are directed to that beloved retirement from which he was drawn by
the voice of millions of freemen, and to which

he now looks for that interval of repose which age and infirmities require. Under these circumstances he ceases to be a subject for the ebullition of the passions, and passes into a character for the contemplation of history.

Historically, then, shall I view him; and limiting this view to his civil administration, I demand, where is there a chief magistrate of whom so much evil has been predicted and from whom so much good has come? Never has any man entered upon the chief magistracy of a country under such appalling predictions of ruin and woe! never has any one been so pursued with direful prognostications! never has any one been so beset and impeded by a powerful combination of political and moneyed confederates! never has any one in any country where the administration of justice has risen above the knife of the bowstring been so lawlessly and shamelessly tried and condemned by rivals and enemies, without hearing, without defense, without the forms of law and justice! History has been ransacked to find examples of tyrants sufficiently odious to illustrate him by comparison. Language has been tortured to find epithets sufficiently strong to paint him in description. Imagination has been exhausted in her efforts to deck him with revolting and inhuman attributes. Tyrant, despot, usurper; destroyer of the liberties of his country; rash, ignorant, imbecile; endangering the public peace with all foreign nations; destroying do-

mestic prosperity at home; ruining all industry, all commerce, all manufactures; annihila-
ting confidence between man and man; deliver-
ing up the streets of populous cities to grass
and weeds, and the wharves of commercial
towns to the encumbrance of decaying vessels;
depriving labor of all reward; depriving industry of all employment; destroying the cur-
rency; plunging an innocent and happy people
from the summit of felicity to the depths of
misery, want, and despair. Such is the faint
outline, followed up by actual condemnation,
of the appalling denunciations daily uttered
against this one MAN, from the moment he became an object of political competition, down to
the concluding moment of his political existence.

The sacred voice of inspiration has told us
that there is a time for all things. There certainly has been a time for every evil that human nature admits of to be vaticinated of President Jackson's administration; equally certain
the time has now come for all rational and
well-disposed people to compare the predictions
with the facts, and to ask themselves if these
calamitous prognostications have been verified
by events? Have we peace or war with foreign nations? Certainly we have peace with all
the world! peace with all its benign, and felici-
tous, and beneficent influences! Are we respected, or despised abroad? Certainly the
American name never was more honored

throughout the four quarters of the globe than in this very moment. Do we hear of indignity or outrage in any quarter? of merchants robbed in foreign ports? of vessels searched on the high seas? of American citizens impressed into foreign service? of the national flag insulted anywhere? On the contrary, we see former wrongs repaired, no new one inflicted. France pays twenty-five millions of francs for spoliations committed thirty years ago; Naples pays two millions one hundred thousand ducats for wrongs of the same date; Denmark pays six hundred and fifty thousand rix-dollars for wrongs done a quarter of a century ago; Spain engages to pay twelve millions of reals vellon for injuries of fifteen years' date; Portugal, the last in the list of former aggressors, admits her liability and only waits the adjustment of details to close her account by adequate indemnity.

From President Jackson the country has first learned the true theory and practical intent of the Constitution in giving to the executive a qualified negative on the legislative power of Congress. Far from being an odious, dangerous, or kingly prerogative, this power as vested in the president is nothing but a qualified copy of the famous veto power vested in the tribunes of the people among the Romans, and intended to suspend the passage of a law until the people themselves should have time to consider it. The qualified veto of the president destroys nothing; it only delays the passage of a law and refers it to the people for their consideration and decision. It is the reference of a law, not to a committee of the House, or of the whole House, but to the committee of the whole Union. It is a recommitment of the bill to the people, for them to examine and consider; and if, upon this examination, they are content to pass it, it will pass at the next session. The delay of a few months is the only effect of a veto in a case where the people shall ultimately approve a law; where they do not approve it, the interposition of the veto is the barrier which saves them the adoption of a law, the repeal of which might afterward be almost impossible. The qualified negative is, therefore, a beneficent power, intended as General Hamilton expressly declares in the *Federalist,* to protect, first, the executive department from the encroachments of the legislative department; and, secondly, to preserve the people from hasty, dangerous or criminal legislation on the part of their representatives.

This is the design and intention of the veto power; and the fear expressed by General Hamilton was that presidents, so far from exercising it too often, would not exercise it as often as the safety of the people required; that they might lack the moral courage to stake themselves in opposition to a favorite measure of the majority of the two Houses of Congress; and thus deprive the people, in many instances, of their right to pass upon a bill before it becomes a final law. The cases in which President Jackson has exercised the veto power have shown the soundness of these observations. No ordinary president would have staked himself against the Bank of the United States and the two Houses of Congress in 1832. It required President Jackson to confront that power—to stem that torrent—to stay the progress of that charter and to refer it to the people for their decision. His moral courage was equal to the crisis. He arrested the charter until it could be got to the people, and they have arrested it for ever. Had he not done so the charter would have become a law and its repeal almost impossible. The people of the whole Union would now have been in the condition of the people of Pennsylvania, bestrode by the monster, in daily conflict with him, and maintaining a doubtful contest for supremacy between the government of a State and the directory of a moneyed corporation.

To detail specific acts which adorn the administration of President Jackson and illustrate the intuitive sagacity of his intellect, the firmness of his mind, his disregard of personal popularity, and his entire devotion to the public good, would be inconsistent with this rapid sketch intended merely to present general views, and not to detail single actions, howsoever worthy they may be of a spendid page in the volume of history. But how can we pass over the great measure of the removal of the public moneys from the Bank of the United States in the autumn of 1833? that wise, heroic, and masterly measure of prevention which has rescued an empire from the fangs of a merciless, revengeful, greedy, insatiate, implacable, moneyed power!

The difficulty with France: what an instance it presents of the superior sagacity of President Jackson over all the commonplace politicians who beset and impede his administration at home! That difficulty, inflamed and aggravated by domestic faction, wore, at one time, a portentous aspect; the skill, firmness, elevation of purpose, and manly frankness of the president avoided the danger, accomplished the object, commanded the admiration of Europe, and retained the friendship of France. He conducted the delicate affair to a successful and mutual honorable issue. All is amicably and happily terminated, leaving not a wound, nor even a scar, behind; leaving the Frenchman and American on the ground on which they have stood for fifty years and should for ever stand—the ground of friendship, respect, good will, and mutual wishes for the honor, happiness, and prosperity of each other.

But why this specification? So beneficent and so glorious has been the administration of this president that where to begin and where to end in the enumeration of great measures would be the embarrassment of him who has his eulogy to make. He came into office the first of generals; he goes out the first of statesmen. His civil competitors have shared the fate of his military opponents; and Washington City has been to the American politicians who have assailed him what New Orleans was to the British generals who attacked his lines. Repulsed! driven back! discomfited! crushed! has been the fate of all assailants, foreign and domestic, civil and military. At home and abroad the impress of his genius and of his character is felt. He has impressed upon the age in which he lives the stamp of his arms, of his diplomacy, and of his domestic policy.

In a word, so transcendent have been the merits of his administration that they have operated a miracle upon the minds of his most inveterate opponents. He has expunged their objections to military chieftains! He has shown them that they were mistaken; that military men were not the dangerous rulers they had imagined, but safe and prosperous conductors of the vessel of state. He has changed their fear into love. With visible signs they admit their error, and, instead of deprecating, they now invoke the reign of chieftains. They labored hard to procure a military successor to the present incumbent; and if their love goes on increasing at the same rate the Republic may be put to the expense of periodical wars to breed a perpetual succession of these chieftains to rule over them and their posterity for ever.

To drop this irony which the inconsistency of mad opponents has provoked, and to return to the plain delineations of historical painting, the mind instinctively dwells on the vast and unprecedented popularity of this president. Great is the influence, great the power, greater than any man ever before possessed in our America, which he has acquired over the public mind.

And how has he acquired it? Not by the arts of intrigue, or the juggling tricks of diplomacy; not by undermining rivals or sacrificing public interests for the gratification of classes or individuals. But he has acquired it, first, by the exercise of an intuitive sagacity which, leaving all book learning at an immeasurable distance behind, has always enabled him to adopt the right remedy at the right time and to conquer soonest when the men of forms and office thought him most near to ruin and despair; next, by a moral courage which knew no fear when the public good beckoned him to go on.

Last, and chiefest, he has acquired it by an open honesty of purpose which knew no concealments; by a straightforwardness of action which disdained the forms of office and the arts of intrigue; by a disinterestedness of motive which knew no selfish or sordid calculation; a devotedness of patriotism which staked everything personal on the issue of every measure which the public welfare required him to adopt. By these qualities and these means he has acquired his prodigious popularity and his transcendent influence over the public mind; and if there are any who envy that influence and popularity let them envy also, and emulate if they can, the qualities and means by which they were acquired.

And now, sir, I finish the task which three years ago I imposed upon myself. Solitary and alone, and amid the jeers and taunts of my opponents I put this ball in motion. The people have taken it up and rolled it forward, and I am no longer anything but a unit in the vast mass which now propels it. In the name of that mass I speak. I demand the execution of the edict of the people; I demand the expurgation of that sentence which the voice of a few senators and the power of their confederate, the Bank of the United States, has caused to be placed on the journal of the Senate, and which the voice of millions of freemen has ordered to be expunged from it.

EMERSON

ON THE AMERICAN SCHOLAR[1]
(1837)

Born in 1803, died in 1882; a Unitarian Clergyman in Boston in 1829–32; began a long career as Lecturer in 1833; settled in Concord in 1834; Editor of *The Dial* in 1842–44.

THE planter, who is *man* sent out into the field to gather food, is seldom cheered by any idea of the true dignity of his ministry. He sees his bushel and his cart and nothing beyond, and sinks into the farmer instead of the *man* on the farm. The tradesman scarcely ever gives an ideal worth to his work, but is ridden by the routine of his craft and the soul is subject to dollars. The priest becomes a form; the attorney, a statute book; the mechanic, a machine; the sailor, a rope of a ship. In this distribution of functions the scholar is the delegated intellect. In the right state he is *man thinking*. In the degenerate state, when the victim of society, he tends to become a mere thinker, or, still worse, the parrot of other men's thinking.

[1] From his Phi Beta Kappa oration, delivered at Cambridge, Massachusetts, on August 31, 1837. Printed here by kind permission of Messrs. Houghton, Mifflin & Co. At this time Emerson had just published "Nature" (September, 1836), and had brought out American editions of Carlyle's "Sartor Resartus" and "Essays." In 1833 Emerson had made his first visit to Carlyle.

In this view of him, as *man thinking,* the theory of his office is contained. Him nature solicits with all her placid, all her monitory pictures; him the past instructs; him the future invites. Is not, indeed, every man a student, and do not all things exist for the student's behoof? And finally is not the true scholar the only true master? But the old oracle said: "All things have two handles; beware of the wrong one." In life too often the scholar errs with mankind and forfeits his privilege. Let us see him in his school and consider him in reference to the main influences he receives.

1. The first in time and the first in importance of the influences upon the mind is that of nature. Every day, the sun; and after sunset, night and her stars. Ever the winds blow; ever the grass grows. Every day men and women conversing, beholding and beholden. The scholar is he of all men whom this spectacle most engages. He must settle its value in his mind. What is nature to him? There is never a beginning, there is never an end to the inexplicable continuity of this web of God, but always circular power returning into itself. Therein it resembles his own spirit, whose beginning, whose ending, he never can find—so entire, so boundless. Far, too, as her splendors shine, system on system shooting like rays, upward, downward, without center, without circumference—in the mass and in the particle, nature hastens to render account of herself to the

mind. Classification begins. To the young mind everything is individual, stands by itself. By and by it finds how to join two things and see in them one nature, then three, then three thousand; and so, tyrannized over by its own unifying instinct, it goes on tying things together, diminishing anomalies, discovering roots running under ground, whereby contrary and remote things cohere and flower out from one stem. It presently learns that since the dawn of history there has been a constant accumulation and classifying of facts. But what is classification but the perceiving that these objects are not chaotic and are not foreign, but have a law which is also a law of the human mind? The astronomer discovers that geometry, a pure abstraction of the human mind, is the measure of planetary motion. The chemist finds proportions and intelligible method throughout matter; and science is nothing but the finding of analogy, identity, in the most remote parts. The ambitious soul sits down before each refractory fact; one after another, reduces all strange constitutions, all new powers, to their class and their law, and goes on for ever to animate the last fiber of organization, the outskirts of nature, by insight.

2. The next great influence into the spirit of the scholar is the mind of the past—in whatever form, whether of literature, of art, of institutions, that mind is inscribed. Books are the best type of the influence of the past, and perhaps we shall get at the truth—learn the amount

of this influence more conveniently—by considering their value alone.

The theory of books is noble. The scholar of the first age received into him the world around; brooded thereon; gave it the new arrangement of his own mind and uttered it again. It came into him, life; it went our from him, truth. It came to him, short-lived actions; it went out from him, immortal thoughts. It came to him, business; it went from him, poetry. It was dead fact; now, it is quick thought. It can stand and it can go. It now endures, it now flies, it now inspires. Precisely in proportion to the depth of mind from which it issued, so high does it soar, so long does it sing.

Or, I might say, it depends on how far the process had gone of transmuting life into truth. In proportion to the completeness of the distillation, so will the purity and imperishableness of the product be. But none is quite perfect. As no air-pump can by any means make a perfect vacuum, so neither can any artist entirely exclude the conventional, the local, the perishable from his book or write a book of pure thought that shall be as efficient in all respects to a remote posterity as to contemporaries, or rather to the second age. Each age, it is found, must write its own books; or, rather, each generation for the next succeeding. The books of an older period will not fit this.

Yet hence arises a grave mischief. The sacredness which attaches to the act of creation—

the act of thought—is transferred to the record. The poet chanting was felt to be a divine man: henceforth the chant is divine also. The writer was a just and wise spirit: henceforth it is settled the book is perfect. As love of the hero corrupts into worship of his statue, instantly the book becomes noxious: the guide is a tyrant. The sluggish and perverted mind of the multitude, slow to open to the incursions of reason, having once so opened, having once received this book, stands upon it and makes an outcry if it is disparaged. Colleges are built on it. Books are written on it by thinkers, not by *man thinking;* by men of talent—that is, who start wrong; who set out from accepted dogmas, not from their own sight of principles. Meek young men grow up in libraries believing it their duty to accept the views which Cicero, which Locke, which Bacon have given, forgetful that Cicero, Locke, and Bacon were only young men in libraries when they wrote these books.

Hence, instead of *man thinking,* we have the bookworm. Hence, the book-learned class who value books as such; not as related to nature and the human constitution, but as making a sort of third estate with the world and the soul. Hence, the restorers of readings—the emendators, the bibliomaniacs of all degrees.

Books are the best of things, well used; abused, among the worst. What is the right use? What is the one end, which all means go to effect? They are for nothing but to inspire.

I had better never see a book than to be warped by its attraction clean out of my own orbit and made a satellite instead of a system. The one thing in the world of value is the active soul. This every man is entitled to; this every man contains within him, altho, in almost all men, obstructed, and as yet unborn. The soul active sees absolute truth, and utters truth, or creates. In this action, it is genius; not the privilege of here and there a favorite, but the sound estate of every man. In its essence it is progressive. The book, the college, the school of art, the institution of any kind, stop with some past utterance of genius. That is good, say they—let us hold by this. They pin me down. They look backward and not forward. But genius looks forward: the eyes of man are set in his forehead, not in his hindhead; man hopes, genius creates. Whatever talents may be, if the man create not, the pure efflux of the Deity is not his; cinders and smoke there may be, but not yet flame. There are creative manners, there are creative actions, and creative words; manners, actions, words—that is, indicative of no custom or authority, but springing spontaneous from the mind's own sense of good and fair.

Undoubtedly there is a right way of reading, so it be sternly subordinated. *Man thinking* must not be subdued by his instruments. Books are for the scholar's idle times. When he can read God directly the hour is too precious to be wasted in other men's transcripts of their readings. But when the intervals of darkness come, as come they must—when the sun is hid and the stars withdraw their shining—we repair to the lamps which were kindled by their ray, to guide our steps to the East again, where the dawn is. We hear that we may speak. The Arabian proverb says: "A fig-tree, looking on a fig-tree, becomes fruitful."

It is remarkable the character of the pleasure we derive from the best books. They impress us with the conviction that one nature wrote and the same reads. We read the verses of one of the great English poets, of Chaucer, of Marvell, of Dryden, with the most modern joy—with a pleasure, I mean, which is in great part caused by the abstraction of all time from their verses. There is some awe mixed with the joy of our surprise when this poet, who lived in some past world, two or three hundred years ago, says that which lies close to my own soul, that which I also had well-nigh thought and said. But for the evidence thence afforded to the philosophical doctrine of the identity of all minds, we should suppose some preestablished harmony, some foresight of soul that were to be, and some preparation of stores for their future wants, like the fact observed in insects who lay up food before death for the young grub they shall never see.

3. There goes in the world a notion that the scholar should be a recluse, a valetudinarian—as unfit for any handiwork or public labor as

a penknife for an ax. The so-called "practical men" sneer at speculative men as if, because they speculate or see, they could do nothing. I have heard it said that the clergy—who are always, more universally than any other class, the scholars of their day—are addressed as women; that the rough, spontaneous conversation of men they do not hear, but only a mincing and diluted speech. They are often virtually disfranchised; and, indeed, there are advocates for their celibacy. As far as this is true of the studious classes, it is not just and wise. Action is with the scholar subordinate, but it is essential. Without it he is not yet a man. Without it thought can never ripen into truth. While the world hangs before the eye as a cloud of beauty, we can not even see its beauty. Inaction is cowardice, but there can be no scholar without the heroic mind. The preamble of thought, the transition through which it passes from the unconscious to the conscious, is action. Only so much do I know as I have lived. Instantly we know whose words are loaded with life, and whose not.

The world—this shadow of the soul, or *other me*—lies wide around. Its attractions are the keys which unlock my thoughts and make me acquainted with myself. I run eagerly into this resounding tumult. I grasp the hands of those next me, and take my place in the ring to suffer and to work, taught by an instinct, that so shall the dumb abyss be vocal with speech. I pierce its order; I dissipate its fear; I dispose of it within the circuit of my expanding life. So much only of life as I know by experience, so much of the wilderness have I vanquished and planted, or so far have I extended my being, my dominion. I do not see how any man can afford, for the sake of his nerves and his nap, to spare any action in which he can partake. It is pearls and rubies to his discourse. Drudgery, calamity, exasperation, want, are instructors in eloquence and wisdom. The true scholar grudges every opportunity of action past by as a loss of power.

If it were only for a vocabulary the scholar would be covetous of action. Life is our dictionary. Years are well spent in country labors; in town, in the insight into trades and manufactures; in frank intercourse with many men and women; in science; in art; to the one end of mastering in all their facts a language by which to illustrate and embody our perceptions. I learn immediately from any speaker how much he has already lived, through the poverty or the splendor of his speech. Life lies behind us as the quarry from whence we get tiles and cope-stones for the masonry of to-day. This is the way to learn grammar. Colleges and books only copy the language which the field and the workyard made.

But the final value of action, like that of books, and better than books, is, that it is a resource. That great principle of undulation in

nature that shows itself in the inspiring and ex-
piring of the breath; in desire and satiety; in
the ebb and flow of the sea; in day and night;
in heat and cold; and as yet more deeply in-
gratified in every atom and every fluid, is known
to us under the name of polarity—these "fits
of easy transmission and reflection," as Newton
called them, are the law of nature because they
are the law of spirit.

The mind now thinks, now acts; and each fit
reproduces the other. When the artist has exhausted his materials, when the fancy no longer
paints, when thoughts are no longer apprehend-
ed, and books are a weariness—he has always the
resource to live. Character is higher than intellect. Thinking is the function. Living is the
functionary. The stream retreats to its source.
A great soul will be strong to live, as well as
strong to think. Does he lack organ or medium
to impart his truths? He can still fall back on
this elemental force of living them. This is a
total act. Thinking is a partial act. Let the
grandeur of justice shine in his affairs. Let the
beauty of affection cheer his lowly roof. Those
"far from fame," who dwell and act with him,
will feel the force of his constitution in the doings and passages of the day better than it can
be measured by any public and designed display.
Time shall teach him that the scholar loses no
hour which the man lives. Herein he unfolds
the sacred germ of his instinct, screened from influence. What is lost in seemliness is gained in

strength. Not out of those on whom systems of education have exhausted their culture comes the helpful giant to destroy the old or to build the new, but out of unhandseled savage nature, out of terrible Druids and berserkers, come at last Alfred and Shakespeare.

I have now spoken of the education of the scholar by nature, by books, and by action. It remains to say somewhat of his duties.

They are such as become *man thinking*. They may all be comprised in self-trust. The office of the scholar is to cheer, to raise, and to guide men by showing them facts amid appearances. He plies the slow, unhonored, and unpaid task of observation. Flamstee and Herschel, in their glazed observatories, may catalog the stars with the praise of all men, and the results being splendid and useful, honor is sure. But he, in his private observatory, cataloging obscure and nebulous stars of the human mind which as yet no man has thought of as such—watching days and months, sometimes, for a few facts; correcting still his old records—must relinquish display and immediate fame. In the long period of his preparation he must betray often an ignorance and shiftlessness in popular arts, incurring the disdain of the able who shoulder him aside. Long he must stammer in his speech; often forego the living for the dead.

Worse yet, he must accept—how often!—poverty and solitude. For the ease and pleasure of treading the old road, accepting the fashions,

the education, the religion of society, he takes
the cross of making his own, and, of course, the
self-accusation, the faint heart, the frequent un-
certainty and loss of time, which are the nettles
and tangling vines in the way of the self-rely-
ing and self-directed; and the state of virtual
hostility in which he seems to stand to society,
and especially to educated society. For all this
loss and scorn, what offset? He is to find consolation in exercising the highest functions of
human nature. He is one who raises himself
from private consideration and breathes and
lives on public and illustrious thoughts. He is
the world's eye. He is the world's heart. He
is to resist the vulgar prosperity that retro-
grades ever to barbarism by preserving and communicating heroic sentiments, noble biographies,
melodious verse, and the conclusions of history.
Whatsoever oracles the human heart, in all
emergencies, in all solemn hours, has uttered as
its commentary on the world of actions—these
he shall receive and impart. And whatsoever
new verdict Reason from her inviolable seat pro-
nounces on the passing men and events of to-
day—this he shall hear and promulgate.

These being his functions, it becomes him to
feel all confidence in himself and to defer never
to the popular cry. He and he only knows the
world. The world of any moment is the merest
appearance. Some great decorum, some fetish
of a government, some ephemeral trade, or war,
or man, is cried up by half mankind and cried

down by the other half, as if all depended upon this particular up or down. The odds are that the whole question is not worth the poorest thought which the scholar has lost in listening to the controversy. Let him not quit his belief that a popgun is a popgun, tho the ancient and honorable of the earth affirm it to be the crack of doom. In silence, in steadiness, in severe abstraction, let him hold by himself; add observation to observation, patient of neglect, patient of reproach; and bide his own time—happy enough if he can satisfy himself alone that this day he has seen something truly. Success treads on every right step.

For the instinct is sure that prompts him to tell his brother what he thinks. He then learns that in going down into the secrets of his own mind he has descended into the secrets of all minds. He learns that he who has mastered any law in his private thoughts is master to that extent of all men whose language he speaks, and of all into whose language his own can be translated. The poet, in utter solitude remembering his spontaneous thoughts and recording them, is found to have recorded that which men in crowded cities find true for them also. The orator distrusts at first the fitness of his frank confessions—his want of knowledge of the persons he addresses—until he finds that he is the complement of his hearers; that they drink his words because he fulfils for them their own nature; the deeper he dives into his priva-

test, secretest presentiment, to his wonder he
finds this is the most acceptable, most public,
and universally true. The people delight in it;
the better part of every man feels: This is my
music; this is myself.

In self-trust all the virtues are comprehended.
Free should the scholar be—free and brave.
Free even to the definition of freedom, "without any hindrance that does not arise out of his
own constitution." Brave; for fear is a thing
which a scholar by his very function puts behind him. Fear always springs from ignorance.
It is a shame to him if his tranquillity, amid
dangerous times, arise from the presumption
that, like children and women, his is a protected
class; or if he seek a temporary peace by the
diversion of his thoughts from politics or vexed
questions, hiding his head like an ostrich in the
flowering bushes, peeping into microscopes, and
turning rhymes, as a boy whistles, to keep his
courage up. So is the danger a danger still; so is
the fear worse. Manlike, let him turn and face
it. Let him look into its eye and search its nature, inspect its origin—see the whelping of this
lion which lies no great way back; he will then
find in himself a perfect comprehension of its
nature and extent; he will have made his hands
meet on the other side and can henceforth defy
it and pass on superior. The world is his who
can see through its pretension. What deafness,
what stone-blind custom, what overgrown error
you behold is there only by sufferance—by your

sufferance. See it to be a lie, and you have already dealt it its mortal blow.

Men such as they are very naturally seek money or power; and power because it is as good as money—the "spoils," so-called, "of office." And why not? for they aspire to the highest, and this, in their sleep-walking, they dream is highest. Wake them, and they shall quit the false good and leap to the true, and leave governments to clerks and desks. This revolution is to be wrought by the gradual domestication of the idea of culture. The main enterprise of the world for splendor, for extent, is the upbuilding of a man. Here are the materials strewn along the ground. The private life of one man shall be a more illustrious monarchy—more formidable to its enemy, more sweet and serene in its influence to its friend than any kingdom in history. For a man, rightly viewed, comprehends the particular natures of all men. Each philosopher, each bard, each actor, has only done for me as by a delegate, what one day I can do for myself. The books which once we valued more than the apple of the eye, we have quite exhausted. What is that but saying that we have come up with the point of view which the universal mind took through the eyes of one scribe; we have seen that man and have passed on. First one, then another; we drain all cisterns, and, waxing greater by all these supplies, we crave a better and more abundant food. The man has never lived that can feed us ever. The human mind can not be enshrined in a person who shall set a barrier on any one side to this unbounded, unboundable empire. It is one central fire, which, flaming now out of the lips of Etna, lightens the capes of Sicily; and, now out of the throat of Vesuvius, illuminates the towers and vineyards of Naples. It is one light which beams out of a thousand stars. It is one soul which animates all men.

END OF VOL. VIII